D1187154

Weimaraner

EDITED BY
PATSY HOLLINGS

ACKNOWLEDGEMENTS

The publishers would like to acknowledge the following for help with photography: David Tomlinson, Pam Thompson (Risinglark), Hearing Dogs for Deaf People, and Pets As Therapy.

Cover photo: © Tracy Morgan Animal Photography (www.animalphotographer.co.uk)
Photographs on pages 6, 18, 26, 52 and 130 © Lynn Kipps (lynn@kipps.co.uk)
page 2 © istockphoto.com/Gualberto Bucerra; page 22 © Ralf Weigel
page 26 © istockphoto.com/Alice Anne Heath; page 38 © istockphoto.com/rotofrank
page 39 © istockphoto.com/Adventure_Photo; page 41 © istockphoto.com/zimmytws
page 100 © istockphoto.com/Cole Vineyard; page 101 © istockphoto.com/Jessi Tetzloff
pages 107 and 111 © istockphoto.com/poco_bw

The British Breed Standard reproduced in Chapter 7 is the copyright of the Kennel Club and published with the club's kind permission. Extracts from the American Breed Standard are reproduced by kind permission of the American Kennel Club.

THE QUESTION OF GENDER
**The 'he' pronoun is used throughout this book instead of the rather impersonal 'it',
but no gender bias is intended.**

First published in 2009 by The Pet Book Publishing Company Limited
PO Box 8, Lydney, Gloucestershire GL15 6YD

ISBN
978-1-906305-16-1
1-906305-16-1

Printed and bound in Singapore.

CONTENTS

GETTING TO KNOW WEIMARANERS

Chapter 1

I n order to understand the Weimaraner first you must understand where he came from and the work he was bred to undertake. The Weimaraner came into being by the selective breeding of the nobles and their breed masters from the former state of Weimar, Germany. He was jealously guarded and highly prized. Because of the secrecy surrounding the development of the breed, there was little documentation to provide continuity of lineage. There were also numerous theories purported by the 'experts' of the day surrounding the possible breeds that could have contributed to the evolution of the Weimaraner. It was not until 1896 that representation by parties with great experience and knowledge of the breed were able to put forward a strong enough argument in favour of the Weimaraner being recognised as a pure breed to gain approval of the Delegate Commission. This was a body of canine experts who were familiar with breeds of the day and were responsible for identifying pure breeds. Their acceptance meant that the Weimaraner became a specific breed, and, from that day, was allowed entry into the German stud book.

Originally, the Weimaraner was bred to hunt in packs.   *lynn@kipps.co.uk*

The Weimaraner was initially conceived as a hunting dog that would hunt in packs and, on occasions, hunt in both pairs and singly. What was needed in this role was the combination of boldness and bravery with intelligence and guile. A dog would be expected to enter virtually impenetrable forest and to cover extremely unforgiving terrain. There he would encounter, and be expected to hunt, bear, deer and wild boar, which are formidable opponents when run to ground. A pack of dogs could work together to bring down the prey, but if only one or two Weimaraners were hunting, the danger was extreme. In this situation, a Weimaraner needed to make use of all his talents. If he showed fear or failure to stand his ground, then he was of no use as a hunting dog. Few dogs were kept as pets in those days, so a failed hunting dog would probably be culled. If, on the other hand, a Weimaraner could out-manoeuvre his quarry, using his keen intelligence and brave disposition, he could deliver the quarry to his owners and become the victor and not the victim.

A CHANGING ROLE

Around the 1920s, the Weimaraner was called on to perform his duties in a different manner, as a result of the changing political and economic climate. World War One had come to an end and the nobility lost their status as the Weimar Republic was formed in 1919. The Weimaraner, the jealously guarded possession of the nobility, lost his protection and became accessible to a wider public. But he was no longer required to hunt large game in extensive forests because this privilege, enjoyed by the nobility, was at an end. The Weimaraner was about to embark on a whole new way of life, joining the ranks of the working gundog. He would no longer be the 'elite' dog of Europe, but eventually his talents would be recognised in countries all over the world.

The Weimaraner learnt to adapt and became a dog that would work under his own initiative. He needed all his intelligence to rise to this new situation. Single dogs and pairs would now be used to find smaller game, which would most likely be killed with the gun or, occasionally, the hawk. This new work meant the Weimaraner was now used to hunt by quartering the ground, using the game scent and wind to cross a large expanse of ground from right to left or left to right, rather than the direct line of running game. While he was carrying out this task he would be expected to

Working practices changed, so the Weimaraner had to adapt to a new role, scenting game and then holding it on point.

David Tomlinson

This is a medium-sized dog, built for stamina rather than speed.

acknowledge scent. In their old guise, a pack of Weimaraners would trail scent on the ground until the animal they were tracking was cornered: they could howl and bay until their masters came to claim their prize. Now when the Weimaraner covered his ground, he would be taking in air scent, carrying his nose higher. Each time he encountered scent, he might just check his stride to indicate to his new master that there was quarry hidden further forward in the field or cover.

The Weimaraner's job was to pick up the scent of small quarry, fox, hare and rabbit plus all the game bird species that would inhabit that terrain, even the waders and wildfowl. Rather than kill the quarry, a Weimaraner was expected to work in close proximity and hold a staunch point. This is when a dog, closing in on a strong game scent, reaches a position where his body freezes, head in line with the quarry and tail rigid with no movement at all. To be motionless is vital: if a dog looks around or edges forward, then it is likely the game is on the move. When both dog and game are still, the dog may hold a front leg bent in classic pointing mode or, like many Weimaraners, he will hold a hind leg. If the game sits tight, then the dog should remain steady until such time as his owner arrives with falcon or gun. He would then flush the game so that the owner could enjoy his sport, the dog remaining calm and steady. This would be followed by a soft-mouthed

retrieve from either land or water.

The sportsmen relied on the intelligence of the Weimaraner to accommodate a series of adaptations, regardless of how alien they were for a breed that was primarily conceived as a hunting dog. The Weimaraner still carries all these diverse attributes. He is bold, fearless, protective, and, when necessary, will use his intelligence and strength to his own advantage.

THE WEIMARANER TODAY

The Weimaraner is now firmly established in the UK and has become one of the top 20 breeds registered by the Kennel Club. It has an even larger following in the USA. *What makes a Weimaraner so special?*

SETTING A STANDARD

Breed Standards were introduced to provide breeders with a guide by which to compare their stock and as a means to measure the quality of dogs being produced. When the original German Standard was interpreted by other countries to produce their own Breed Standards, it would seem that either poor translation or misunderstanding caused anomalies that would have the potential to provide a certain diversity of breed type.

This area is covered in more detail in Chapter 7, so I will only provide a few examples to clarify the point.

The UK Breed Standard calls for the Weimaraner to be equal when measured floor to withers and withers to tail, the FCI (European Standard), calls for a measurement ratio of 11 high and 12 long. The UK Breed Standard asks that the quarters have **moderate angulation with a well turned stifle**, the AKC (American Kennel Club) Breed Standard requires quarters to be **well angulated**. It is easy to see why there is diversity in breed type between each country but it is also fair to say that not all breeders achieve all aspects of their own Breed Standard and therefore type will be diverse within each country.

GENERAL APPEARANCE

The Weimaraner is one of the larger breeds in the Hunt, Point Retrieve (HPR) group, although he is classified as a medium-sized working gundog. The correct size range in the United Kingdom should be, dogs 24-27 inches (61-69 cms) and 22-25 inches (56-64 cms) for bitches at the withers. General appearance is that of a medium-sized dog that has good bone and depth throughout, the deep chest providing good lung capacity, ribcage extending well back, retaining good depth in the loin area. This is the build of a dog bred for stamina rather than speed over the shorter distances.

THE HEAD

The true Weimaraner head is a joy to behold, embellished with fine detail of layered muscle, prominent veining on the cheeks and defined bone structure on the skull, giving rise to the 'aristocratic' title that best described such quality. The best heads have now been lost to the breed and generally today can be described as 'good' or otherwise. A summarised description would be as follows:

Nose delicate and wide in nostril to take in the game scent, colour should the same as the underside of a fresh mushroom just opening. The foreface should be straight and wide enough to allow good passage of scent, only

The classic Weimaraner head, with its distinctive aristocratic appearance.   lynn@kipps.co.uk

a moderate stop. The skull should be rounded showing brain room, neither too wide nor too narrow. Ears set high on the head, wide with a definite fold, velvet thin and yet still durable enough to go through thick cover. There are arches just behind the eyes that add character and definition to the skull. The eyes are blue in tiny puppies and become lighter at the juvenile stages. Normally they would become amber at around two and a half years old. Looking into the eyes they should be medium-sized, round, bright and alive; the amber gives the expression a softness, but they must look back at you. They convey a confident and questioning expression. There is a visible alertness, a readiness for whatever is to come next.

THE COLOUR

One of the first things that people notice about the Weimaraner is his arresting colour, which is described as shades of silver, roe or mouse grey. The preferred colour is silver-grey, ideally with a metallic sheen.

The Weimaraner is often referred to as the 'grey ghost', and this conveys the impression of something seen on the moors in *Wuthering Heights*. However, it is important not to be taken in by this romantic idea, or to choose the breed solely because of its stunning colour. The Weimaraner is not the easiest breed to own, and demands special understanding. It is akin to the spider's web; insects become attracted to the web only to realise when it is too late that there is a lot more hidden there. People choose a Weimaraner for the unusual colour and when they get home they are suddenly faced with the reality that this is an all-action breed. The Weimaraner uses his brain to try to gain advantage over the owner. He may become wilful, stubborn and sometimes downright disobedient. The fact that the Weimaraner is so intelligent is the reason why he is so highly valued by the dedicated owner, and why he is the cause of so much frustration among the uninitiated.

The 'grey ghost' tag refers mainly to the action while

TAILS WIN

The first imports arrived in the UK and were docked. For many years the Breed Standard referred to the Weimaraner as a customarily docked breed. The tail was removed at around three days old so that the remainder when extended should cover the scrotum in dogs and the vulva in bitches. The thickness should be in proportion to the body and it should be carried normally in line with the back. Too high and it was felt that temperament might be a bit too much, i.e. on his toes and ready for action, the tail carried too low, between the legs and the dog maybe too sensitive and reserved, not of true character. These comments refer to a dog on the move not just standing around. Longhairs had just the tip of the tail removed.

The practice of docking was not just about tradition, it was both to maintain the Breed Standard as we know it, and to prevent damage to tails which would thrash around when working in dense cover. Recently the law and the Breed Standard have changed in the UK and tails are no longer docked unless a dog is a working gundog. The undocked tail should reach down to the hocks and taper towards the tip. It should be carried below the line of the back when relaxed and may be raised when a dog is excited, but should never be carried over the back. Weimaraners that continue to be used for work are still permitted to be docked but now this requires proof of the intention to work and the procedure must be carried out by a veterinary surgeon, certified and the dog micro-chipped. These dogs will no longer be allowed to be exhibited at shows where the public pay to gain admission.

Legislation means that it is now illegal to dock tails unless the dog is a working gundog. *lynn@kipps.co.uk*

The longhaired Weimaraner is an exact counterpart of the shortcoated variety, with the exception of the length of coat. *Keith Allison.*

working in the half light. If you have been shooting and walk home at dusk, you may see the Weimaraner out in front suddenly disappearing, only to re-appear from out of nowhere. Then, just as you bring the dog into focus, he seems to float from your vision. It is an experience, certainly, but not a reason to buy a Weimaraner.

THE COAT

There are shorthaired and longhaired variants of the breed. The shorthaired Weimaraner has a smooth sleek coat, often described as having a metallic sheen. It should not feel unnecessarily harsh to the touch, nor should it be wiry; it should be dense, smooth and sleek. It was claimed once upon a time that people with allergies could own the Weimaraner. In the early days of the breed, dogs would have been kept in outside kennels, and these tougher living conditions meant that the coat did not shed to any great extent and that is perhaps why the stories came about. However, now that the Weimaraner is primarily a companion dog kept

inside (with all the benefits of central heating, double glazing and cosier beds with synthetic bedding), he does shed his coat and the advice previously given regarding those with allergies should now be viewed with a degree of scepticism. Remember, the Weimaraner is a breed that is made of myth and legend.

The longhaired Weimaraner, as the name suggests, has a coat that is longer on the body than the smooth – 1-2 inches (2.5-5 cms), even longer still on the neck, chest and belly. There is feathering on the ears, chest, tail and the back of each leg. But with the exception of the coat, the appearance of a longhaired Weimaraner should be identical to the shortcoated variety. As with the shorthaired, feet should be webbed.

If you are thinking of owning a Weimaraner then clearly there is much to consider. Breeding is not a science but an art. It may well become a science in the future when the scientists perfect their cloning techniques. But while there are so many variables, breeding, for now, remains an art. I have had many conversations with other breeders over the years, some of these going well into the night, mainly concerning inherited defects, genetic pre-disposition, even inbreeding coefficients. If breeding were as simple as ruling out all dogs with any genetic fault, hereditary defect and any anti-social traits, it would be so much simpler for all of us. Some breeders take that simplicity to the most unimaginative levels.

They take their average bitch to be mated to a well-known stud dog just because he is the current top winner, and expect him to imprint all his virtues without any vices on all the resulting offspring.

SO WHAT SHOULD YOU EXPECT?

The breed still holds fast to the 'dual purpose' aspects for which it was bred, but breeders provide their own input into the construction and inherent characteristics of the breed. Some breeders may believe that breeding from purely working lines increases their chances of owning a dog with only the very best attributes for work. For competitive fieldwork it is imperative to have acute scenting ability, and to improve their chances of competing, a fast, stylish and thorough worker that excels at retrieving on both land and in water. Consider the expectations of those early pioneers, taking into account that the breed's working ability and exploits had become almost legend to those who had witnessed his prowess before importation began.

The Weimaraner has now been in the UK for more than 50 years and breeders are still striving to attain a level of consistency and achievement in fieldwork that continues to elude the majority of competitors. The breed has proved itself to be capable of producing top winners in the field, obedience and other elements of work in the US. It

The Weimaraner retains strong working instincts. *David Tomlinson*

could be that the requirements in the UK relating to the style and standard of work might vary from that of America. It might also be that the trainers in the UK are just not maximising the tremendous learning potential or dealing with the strong character that requires a discussion before each command is carried out. Whatever the reason the breed has not reached its full potential, which means that there are tremendous opportunities for new owners to explore and enjoy when owning the Weimaraner.

In the vast majority of cases a well-bred Weimaraner with a diverse family history and without any specific emphasis being placed on competitive attributes is still capable, with competent training, to act as game finder for the owner that shoots or acts as a beater providing game for others. Those same animals could be easily

adapted to agility, working trials and working tests. The nucleus of the breed is still roundly bred using the available diversity of breeding lines. There are a few breeders that adhere to their own principles of breeding from dogs of their own lines, believing that they produce a certain type that fits the Breed Standard well.

If you have not yet purchased your Weimaraner, please remember that if you want to show your dog, you should mention this to your breeder before purchase. While a diversely bred Weimaraner will work in all aspects to a certain level of performance, if you have any serious detrimental faults, such as a large white marking on the chest, a bad mouth, or in a dog if he were a monorchid, (only one testicle descended into the scrotum), then you do not have a dog that could compete at any serious level of showing.

VERSATILE WEIMERANERS

If you have already purchased your Weimaraner, you should be aware of what you have taken on. That means you need to find out how your dog is bred in order to fully understand his capabilities. A distinct advantage of owning the Weimaraner is that owners can participate in a number of activities. The Weimaraner is one of the most versatile workers, not just within the HPR section but in the whole of the gundog group.

It is true that the Weimaraner does have limitations that inhibit his ability to attain the highest qualifications in certain disciplines. For instance, in field trial competitions it is widely known that the Weimaraner is a thorough and diligent worker, but he is quite often penalised for lack of pace. When you consider the speed and free-ranging capacity of others in the HPR section the criticism may be justified in some cases. Weimaraners for all their adaptability will never be as fast or precise in obedience as the Border Collie.

In working trials, the Weimaraner is extremely well suited. As a big, bold dog he can excel at long jumps and scales, and he is in his element on the tracking. But as a soft-mouthed

This is a breed that can perform to a high standard in many of the canine disciplines.

gundog he will not (and I hope will never) be as sharp on the manwork as the German Shepherd, although the Weimaraner has been used by the police for general dog work duties and as a 'sniffer' dog. If you decide that competing with your Weimaraner is not for you, you can train him to be a PAT (pets as therapy) dog, visiting residential and care homes for the elderly and providing them with the opportunity to enjoy the temporary companionship of a friendly dog, providing stimulation, therapy and diversity in their daily routine. Wherever intelligence, adaptability and a bold brave attitude are required then there will be opportunities for the Weimaraner.

AN IDEAL HOME

The Weimaraner is a medium-sized, energetic dog, and it is important to make sure you can provide a suitable home for this highly intelligent breed.

There is no ideal home or owner for a Weimaraner. I have visited owners with acres of ground and the dogs were all running free. Perfect, you might think, but only if you also spend time with each dog individually. A Weimaraner needs to be part of your life; he loves people and enjoys interacting with them. He is a good family dog and once he understands your routine and where he fits in with that daily pattern, he will become contented.

I have witnessed this contentment first hand with dogs living in a terraced property with just a backyard. Weimaraners need the routine and the basic discipline that allows them to stay within the boundaries set by their owners, and they need work of some description for stimulation. The perfect home would be one that could offer all of the above in a loving environment. I personally would not be happy for a Weimaraner to spend all his life in an apartment, as this is a breed that needs outside space for relaxation and freedom. There is no clear advantage of country over town living, providing the dog enjoys a full, active, stimulating life with a close and loving family where he is an integral part of their family life.

The Weimaraner is not in the strictest sense of the word a playful breed. He can and will play on occasions like any other dog. He likes to choose his own friends and can appear standoffish. However, if he is left alone, he will come round to greeting visitors if they can be patient.

LIVING WITH CHILDREN

Do not allow children to pull a puppy around. A puppy – and an adult dog – will appreciate some quiet time, so when your Weimaraner goes off to his bed to rest, do not allow children or anyone to disturb him. The Weimaraner is a family dog, who wants and needs to be involved in all aspects of your home life. To get to that point, however, means that he cannot have free rein to do as he would like. He needs training in order to understand and adapt to the family routine. This will need to include all members of the family. Children are usually the most difficult to bring into the programme because they see the dog as a friend and playmate. Owners must therefore provide the initial discipline for both dog

A Weimaraner can fit into most homes, as long as he is an integral part of family life.

and child, so that mutual respect is established.

MORE THAN ONE

Can Weimaraners get on with other dogs? The answer is yes – you only have to see well-adjusted, working dogs travelling together in a cattle truck when they are out on a shoot. Temperament has got to be perfect, as the dogs lie over each other and have people squashing them together in very close proximity to other dogs.

However, I would not advise inexperienced people to introduce a male Weimaraner into a home where there is another male dog. It does not matter what type of dog we are talking about –

without experienced owners, it is likely to be a recipe for disaster. The Weimaraner will not readily accept domination from another male dog. Where two dogs must live in close proximity, it is vital that owners can read the signs of a dog trying to assert himself over his companion.

LIVING WITH OTHER ANIMALS

Weimaraners will get along with most other animals, the important thing is to consider how best to introduce them. Over the years children's pets have expanded from the cats, rabbits, hamsters and mice of my boyhood, to rats, gerbils, chipmunks and a wide array of other mammals and reptiles. A Weimaraner puppy knows no boundaries with other animals so it is imperative that owners provide the discipline required for a smooth transition with other pets.

EXERCISE

The adult dog will take whatever exercise you want to give him. Personally, I do not think that exercise is the key to making a good companion. You would be better employed establishing a solid routine around your lifestyle.

Once the Weimaraner understands your routine and accepts where he fits into it, he will become a dog at ease with his

THE STORY OF RYAN

If ownership of the Weimaraner sounds a little daunting, I am walking proof that even from bad experiences lessons can be learned. My first Weimaraner, Ryan, was totally loyal to me and I was totally committed to him. We went everywhere together – weddings, funerals, family parties, in fact any invitation that was received without the extended invitation to Ryan was discarded. After some basic training we entered a Championship obedience class and this is where I learnt my first lesson. Having executed the basic tests, losing only one mark, we went for the retrieve of a dumbbell. Ryan went out and collected the article with ease, he turned to return

and the look on his face said it all: "I have the dumbbell, you know you will get the dumbbell, what more do you want, gift wrapping?" He was so slow on his return that we were heavily penalised and out of contention.

Undeterred we entered a working test to assess his fieldwork potential. I remember on that day we were firing on all cylinders. Blind and memory retrieves, directional control, all were fine. We came to a simple and straightforward retrieve of a dummy from over a field gate. The dummy was thrown, the dog was sent. Instead of him clearing the gate by a couple of feet as he always did in training, he went under the gate, ignored the

lifestyle. Exercise forms part of his day but does not become his sole expectation, therefore he will accept that his rest time, stimulation, and meal times all form part of his overall day.

TRAINABILITY

The Breed Standard tells us that the breed should be **fearless, friendly, protective and obedient**. Remembering what the breed was developed for (to hunt bear, deer and boar), it is understandable that the true character and temperament of the Weimaraner should be bold and outgoing. But he is also highly trainable and adaptable.

The breed is inherently protective. The Weimaraner is a thinking dog and because of this

he will protect your home and property. He would not normally rush into a protection situation by attacking any intruder; he is more likely to threaten the perpetrator with a deep growl and by raising his hackles. If the intruder failed to withdraw and posed a more serious threat, a Weimaraner would then defend you and your property.

This does not mean he is an easy breed to train – far from it. The intelligent Weimaraner can take advantage of a person who is unfamiliar with breed-specific training methods. See Chapter Six: Training and Socialisation

THE RIGHT CHOICE

Ownership of this breed is not for the faint-hearted. If you are a

committed dog owner, and you are prepared to have your life changed completely, then a Weimaraner could be the breed for you. If, on the other hand you want a dog that you give a warm, comfortable bed, a walk around the block twice a day and then expect him to sleep until fed, perhaps a different choice would be a better option for you.

In many ways, the Weimaraner is a high-maintenance breed. If you weigh up all the work and effort you put in, you will get back tenfold-frustration, annoyance, stubbornness, and in equal measure, love, dedication and unquestioning loyalty. It sounds like a good bargain to me.

dummy, and made his way to another test where he unceremoniously urinated over a judge's coat which was hung over the back of a chair. Needless to say, we did not win the test.

My first venture into the shooting world was even more embarrassing. I was invited to join in on a local shooting day. I had no idea about dog work so kept Ryan on the lead. The organiser had a quiet word saying, 'you will never know how he can work on a lead, you must let him off'. I obediently complied and Ryan went off at full speed enjoying his new-found freedom. He accelerated down a wide ride and suddenly crashed into two of the guns and three beaters who were quietly walking and talking their way to their positions. He hit the two shooters squarely behind the knees and they crumpled, bringing down the beaters like dominoes. They all leapt up screaming profanities.

Weimaraners raise your expectations and quite often they take your spirits to new heights, then without any malice, just by doing something that would be so simple to them, they become the clown and suddenly your expectations are shattered. I remember those and many other occasions with great fondness. If ever there was a reason for owning a Weimaraner then a lifetime of fun and memories must surely be the one.

SUMMING UP

I have enjoyed many Weimaraners, all different in so many ways. We have achieved an understanding and all of my experiences have been beneficial to me and so rewarding. I have learned to love this breed with a passion. I awake every day and I am grateful that as I walk into my kitchen I am greeted by my seven current Weimaraners.

This is just the start; the entertainment, involvement and satisfaction they provide carries on throughout the day. Every day for me is a joy living with Weimaraners and has been for the last 36 years. Enjoy your Weimaraner, never abuse him, cherish his company but steel your heart for when you lose him.

The Weimaraner can be a challenging breed to own, but you will be rewarded with countless happy memories.

THE FIRST WEIMARANERS

Chapter 2

It has long been expounded that the Weimaraner was developed at the court of the city of Weimar, in the province of Thuringia in Germany, by Grand Duke Karl August (1757-1827) around 1775. Many theories abound regarding the Weimaraner's origins and the breeds that may, or may not, have contributed to the structure and temperament of the dogs as we know them today.

GERMAN OR FRENCH?

In the 14th century, at the French court of Louis IX, there lived a pack of grey dogs called the Chien Gris de Saint Louis, most probably imported from Egypt. Louis had become fascinated by their ability to track large game. At that time, hunting was all the rage, so it was not uncommon for great hunting dogs to be given as presents among the French noblemen – thus the dogs were distributed throughout France. In time these dogs were prevalent in most other European countries and were highly prized for their working ability.

The stunning painting *Le Livre de la Chasse* by Gaston Phoebus (Gaston III, Count of Fois)[1], who lived from 1331 until 1391, portrays these Chien Gris de Saint Louis in multiple aspects. But it was not just their colour that distinguished them from all other hunting dogs. This type of dog had flat cheeks, light eyes, an eel stripe along its spine, high-set, long ears with a distinctive fold at the front edge, a median line running from occiput to nose, and a tail with a curl. These features are displayed in modern-day Weimaraners although the curl in the tail has been obscured due to docking.

Three different categories of hunting dogs existed in the 14th century:

- **Alaunt:** a fierce, fast dog capable of bringing down any large game.
- **Levrier:** almost Greyhound in shape and colouring, and used as a sighthound.
- **Courant (running):** these dogs had full, broad muzzles and long pendulous ears and were used as scenthounds.

The Chien Gris de Saint Louis was the elite of the Courant dogs. Worked on-lead and housed separately from the other hunting dogs, these dogs lived in the homes of their handlers. It is easily understood that a great dependence and bond would have been formed between these medieval dogs and humans. Is this the forerunner of the strong dog-to-human bond that exists in our modern Weimaraner? If so, then this has been maintained throughout the Weimaraner's evolution for more than 600

Hunting dogs were originally used on larger animals, such as wild boar, but, in time, there was a need for a finer 'bird' dog.
David Tomlinson

years and must be recognised, and accepted, as an integral part of the breed's instinct and history.

Throughout the 15th and 16th centuries, the Chien Gris de Saint Louis maintained its popularity among the royal courts and was frequently featured in tapestries and paintings of the time. Notable among these is the *Wild Boar Hunt* by Jost Amman (1539-1591), which portrays three silver-grey dogs with the typical ear fold. Although born in Switzerland, Jost Amman spent a great deal of his life living in Nuremberg, so this may well be the first evidence of the dogs in Germany.

Come the 17th century, for some reason the Chien Gris (or Grey Dog) lost its popularity in favour of white dogs, although it is in 1632 that the Flemish artist Van Dyck painted a portrait of Prinz Rupprecht von der Pfalz with a Weimaraner-coloured 'Huehnerhund' sitting at his feet. While the stop is much more exaggerated than in modern Weimaraners, the long ears and distinctive fold are clearly visible.

Although popularity had waned, there is evidence in the paintings of Jean Baptiste Oudry that the Chien Gris de Saint Louis still existed in France come the 18th century. With the introduction of firearms in the mid 1800s, there was a need for the lighter-built Pointer-type dog that was keener on birds than on large game. In the UK, breeding lines followed this path but the Europeans maintained breeding lines of a more versatile nature and this continued through to the 19th century.

It is during the turn of the 19th century that we hear of

Grand Duke Karl August's involvement with the Weimaraner. Both Strebel and Friess, prolific authors of dog books at the time, mentioned the versatile Weimaraner, its hunting prowess and the extensive numbers in Thuringia. Were the dogs owned by Grand Duke Karl August descendants of the original Chien Gris de Saint Louis? Had Karl August succeeded in maintaining a pure strain in order to retain their hunting characteristics?

Karl August was the highest ruling nobleman at the court of Weimar and held the veto on who could, or could not, own a Weimaraner. As only the ruling classes were, by law, allowed to own hunting dogs, his decision would have been based on the hierarchical position of a member of his, or another, court. He was extremely secretive about his dogs and their breeding, which has unfortunately denied us any knowledge of them. Records and archives are unavailable and/or have been destroyed, possibly to maintain the mystery.

Through the art and literature of the 19th century, evidence continued to mount when, in 1850, Joseph Kidd, one of the founding members of the Royal Scottish Academy of Painting, Sculpture and Architecture, portrayed a dog in an oil painting, simply entitled *Weimaraner*. This painting most closely resembles our modern-day Weimaraner, complete with docked tail.

Numbers gradually increased, and, some 32 years later, the Thuringia Club for Breeding Purebred Dogs is reported as having a 'strong representation' of Weimaraners.

BREED DEVELOPMENT

It was not until the beginning of the 20th century that theories of the breed's origins became rife – one being that Grand Duke Karl August had decided to create the breed himself. Other theories attempted to prove that the breed was developed through specific cross-breeding, with the Pointer, the Spanish Pointer, the German Shorthaired Pointer, the Great Dane, the Saint Hubertus Bracke, the Bloodhound and the Leithund/Schweisshund all being included. Once the geneticists could identify how coat colour was inherited, the majority of these theories could be dismissed.

POINTER/SPANISH POINTER

There were diverse and differing opinions as to whether crosses with either, or both, the Pointer or the Spanish Pointer helped to create the foundations of the Weimaraner. Dr August Stroese, a notable authority on dogs, commented in 1902:

"The silver grey Weimaraner is said to be descended from a yellow and white, smooth-haired English Pointer bitch, imported into Germany in the 1820s by the Duke of Weimar and crossbred with German dogs".[2]

In addition, Brandt stated that it was Grand Duke Karl August who mated a German Shorthaired Pointer to a Pointer, producing in the litter a grey dog, which was the foundation of the Weimaraner breed. This theory gained little acceptance, as it did not explain how the Weimaraner or 'Chien Gris' was transformed from a tracking hound into a dog that hunted bird and small game.

Pointer: An English Pointer may have been used in the development of the Weimaraner.

German Shorthaired Pointer: Note the marked contrast in head shape with the Weimaraner.

Great Dane: Note the flat cheeks, which are similar to a Weimaraner's.

GERMAN SHORTHAIRED POINTER

Being two German dogs, it could have been assumed there was a genetic closeness through cross-breeding between the German Shorthaired Pointer and the Weimaraner. However, structural differences in the two breeds make this unlikely. The Weimaraner is a much longer dog than the German Shorthaired Pointer and the heads are completely different. Regardless, a gentleman known as R.F. expounded this theory of intermingling by suggesting that the alteration in colour resulted from a vitamin deficiency.

R.F.'s theory was ultimately discredited in an article written by Major Robert aus der Herber in 1936. He stated:

"…but as it has been proved that two black animals can produce grey ones, it seems best to look at black ancestors in the old period. There was one black breed, the Saint Hubertus Bracken (sic) amongst the dogs used for hunting in the old days… At the time, a dog breeder seemed to like these grey mutations, he paired them and gradually these dogs appeared in larger numbers here in Thuringia."[3]

GREAT DANE

Interestingly, Dr Paul Kleeman, a grandson of a Weimaraner breeder yet more well known for his knowledge of German Shorthaired Pointers, somehow concluded that the Weimaraner was descended from the blue Great Dane. He had observed the flat cheeks common on both breeds, but, according to his critics, had failed to distinguish between the definite blue of the Great Dane and the grey of the Weimaraner. Dr Kleeman's theory gained no support at the time.

However, this sporting writer

of the 1800s wrote: "By the beginning of the 1880s the Weimaraner was known as the king of hunting dogs and an ornament of classical hunting".

LEITHUND/SCHWEISSHUND

The writer known only as 'Fama' put forward the following theory in an old hunting book:

"The ideal hunting dog in old times was the so-called Leithund (leading dog). This dog was set on the scent of a chosen, not wounded, stag or other deer in the herd and was able to lead the hunter to this single animal. For this purpose, the breed developed the 'Schweisshund' brown colour. Then they had Pointers for smaller game, for birds, rabbits and so forth. Then came the idea to cross these races to meld the hunting qualities of both. The 'Weimaraner' was the result of this noble experiment, a dog that points with exceedingly good nose."[4]

SAINT HUBERTUS BRACKE

A black and tan dog, the probable forerunner of the Bloodhound, but extinct as a breed around the 19th century, this tracking hound was probably the earliest known pure breed – possibly as early as the 8th century. Bred and reared by the monks of the Saint Hubert Abbey in France, in the region of Ardennes, these hounds were well known for their exceptional tracking ability.

According to Beckman, a 16th century writer:

"The Saint Hubertus hounds were often used as lead dogs for black game (wild boar)... Toward the end

Treff von Sandersleben bred by M.F. Pitschke.

of the reign of Louis XIV (1643-1715), they could be seen only with some aristocrats from the north of France who preferred them to all other breeds because they would hunt every type of game".[5]

The Bracke ancestry may well explain the tan markings seen infrequently even in modern day Weimaraners. Although it must be assumed that there were crosses with 'bird' dogs, whether intentional or otherwise, the dilution gene (the gene that contributes to the 'fading' to grey) from the Chien Gris de Saint Louis remained evident along with the structural traits: the broad skull, flat cheeks, ear length with front fold and a tail with a curl. One, or some, of these crosses may well have introduced the longhair gene that remains in the breed and is part of the breed.

BREED RECOGNITION

Established in 1880, the German Delegate Commission received a request for the official recognition of Weimaraners as a breed in its own right. There was significant opposition to this request, mainly claiming that the Weimaraner was simply a German Shorthaired Pointer in a different colour. However, despite these claims, official recognition was awarded in 1896. Even before this award, a Breed Standard had been published in 1894 with The Club for Pure Breeding of Silver Grey Weimaraner Pointers being formed in 1897 to be renamed The Club for the Breeding of the Weimaraner Pointer and later known as The German Weimaraner Club.

After all the dedicated breeding, mainly by Grand Duke Karl August and those who followed him within the German Weimaraner Club, the First World War more or less wiped out Weimaraners in Germany, leaving fewer than a dozen dogs in existence. Recovery was slow but, with the dedication of breeders such as Pitschke (Sandersleben), Wittekop (Rudemanns) and Lindblohm (Lindblohm), the breed started to spread throughout Europe.

The President of the German Weimaraner Club from 1921 to 1946 was Major Robert aus der Herber and the Club's motto stated: 'It is not the breed, but the breeder's selection that guarantees highest quality of conformation and best performance.' This conjoined the dog's structure with its ability to perform and can still hold true today. These post-war breeders bred true to the motto, ensuring that the quality was retained.

After the First World War, breeders had worked hard to re-establish the breed. The Second World War had a severe impact with all organisations coming under government control. After the war Germany was divided and the occupying forces had banned all civilians from owning

OUT OF GERMANY

It was in 1929 that the first pair of Weimaraners set foot on American soil. Howard Knight experienced difficulties persuading the German Weimaraner Club that he was serious about, and committed to, the breed, before he was allowed to import a pair. These were the dog Cosack von Krebitzstein, and the bitch Lotte von Bangstede. Unbeknown to him, the pair had been neutered by radiation before leaving Germany. Knight was more interested in their hunting ability and he used them as working dogs for many years.

Although it took another nine years before he was allowed to import breeding stock, Knight was not to be deterred and finally, just before World War Two, he managed to import several young puppies. Distemper took all but Mars aus der Wulfsriede.

However, soon afterwards, Knight imported Aura von Gaiberg, Adda von Schwarzen Kamp and Dora von Schwarzen Kamp.

In 1939, Knight decided to stop hunting and gave three of his dogs to Margaret and Gus Horn. These were Mars aus der Wulfsriede, Aura von Gaiberg and Adda von Schwarzen Kamp. These became the foundation stock for the

Horns' Grafmar affix.

The Weimaraner Club of America was formed in 1943. As this was during World War Two, the emphasis was on showing and breeding, as hunting had been restricted. The same year saw the first class for Weimaraners being held in Madison Square Gardens. The Best Dog was Grafmar's Kreutz CD and Best Bitch was Grafmar's Diana. Later that year, these two became the first American Champions of the breed, Kreutz managing to beat Diana to that honour by just one day.

The imported Aura von Gaiberg won the first obedience title, known in the United States as CD (Companion Dog). This is totally different from the CD title in Britain and, although there are some elements of agility in the American CD, the emphasis is generally more on obedience.

In the post-war period, there was a speedy influx of exceptional German and Austrian Weimaraners. To maintain quality, the American Kennel Club would only register 'foreign listed' dogs after they had won 10 points in the show ring. Many of these imports left a superb legacy for the future – none more so than Ch. Dido von firearms. Therefore, the hunting tests, used to determine Weimaraners as being fit to breed, came to an abrupt end. As a result, many Weimaraners were exported.

When the allied restrictions on gun ownership were removed, the German Weimaraner Club was reorganised in 1951 and, in 1952, permission to hunt was granted.

FROM GERMANY TO AUSTRIA

The record of how Prinz Hans von Ratibor of Austria came to see the Weimaraner is vague. However, he was extremely well known in hunting circles, both in Germany and Austria, so it was probably during one of these trips that he first met and became fascinated by the Weimaraner. Inspired by his enthusiasm, his friend and employee, Otto von Stockmayer, imported a bitch, Adda von Artlande, from Germany.

Prince Hans von Ratibor owned the Grafenegg estates where he ran hunting tests. In 1921 he imported a pair of Weimaraners from Germany and he was so impressed by them that, after that year, only Weimaraners were allowed to hunt on his estates.

AND INTO AMERICA

Lechsteinhof and his progeny, who all excelled in the field. It was said that to win well in the field, Dido had to be in the pedigree.

However, the most influential of the German imports were those from the Harrasburg lines and these still appear in most Weimaraner extended pedigrees in the United States. In 1949, Bert von der Harrasburg arrived in America. Winning his show title easily, he entered field competition, becoming the first Weimaraner to win an Open All-Age Stake.

By the 1960s, there were few imports with the notable exception of Bella von der Reiteralm. She was bred to Ch. Val Knight Ranck BROM (Breed Record of Merit) who himself was a grandson of Alto von der Harrasburg. Bella, together with the influence of the Harrasburg line, brought to the breed the structural soundness and hunting instinct so important to the breed.

Through her son, Ch. Maximilian von der Reiteralm NSD (Novice Shooting Dog) BROM, 56 Champions were sired, including two dual Champions. Maximilian is the great-grandfather of the British dog Ch. Reeman Aruac CDex, UDex, WDex, TDex, proving that exceptional working ability goes on for generations.

THE BLUE WEIMARANER

As it is a part of the American history, the row over the 'blue' Weimaraner must be briefly mentioned. As with all controversies, there were two sides to the story: those advocating that the colour was the result of a crossbreeding, possibly with a Dobermann, and, on the opposing side, others advocating that it was the result of mutant genes. Either way, it all started with the imported dog Casar von Gaiberg who was, allegedly, the son of a mother/son mating.

Dr Werner Petrie, the 'father' of Weimaraners in Germany, described Casar as having a "touch of black over the entire back, hair very short, eyes not of pure amber colour." His verdict was that the dog was "useless for breeding, most likely a Dobermann cross." When used at stud, Casar's dominant blue trait was evident in all the progeny.

There was such concern among Weimaraner Club of America members that, in 1953, the Breed Standard was changed to disqualify a black mottled mouth, which was always evident in blues. By 1971, such was the disquiet that the American Kennel Club revised the Standard to disqualify blues from show competition. There seemed little uproar from the breeders of blues and the numbers then declined sharply.

Otto himself was a well-known dog show judge and had, at one time, the most authentic documents on the history of the breed. What happened to those records after the Second World War cannot be determined.

In 1935, a longhaired Weimaraner bitch, Donna von Diendorf, was bred by the Countess Stubenburg of Austria. Donna's parents, Gift von Rundhof and Lia Grafenegg, were both shorthaired. Both the sire and the dam can be seen in extended British pedigrees through Donna's litter sister, Dita von Diendorf. With many of the Austrian Weimaraners being longhaired, the Grafenegg affix of Prinz Hans von Ratibor appears regularly in the pedigrees of quality longhairs.

FROM GERMANY TO BRITAIN

The allied forces placed stringent restrictions on Germany after the end of World War Two with a ban on firearms, showing and hunting. This, coupled with the very few remaining Weimaraners in the country, meant that it became all important to resurrect the breed, more for quantity than quality. Interest developed in selling as many Weimaraners as possible to the occupying forces. It was not until 1951 that the restrictions were lifted and the German Weimaraner Club could be reformed.

Members of the committee were horrified that so many of the breed were being exported, so they ruled that no more than half a litter could leave Germany. This allowed the numbers of Weimaraners in Germany to increase and for the breed to be re-established.

While in the army in Germany, Major R.H. Petty, later to establish the Strawbridge affix, and Major Eric Richardson, whose affix was Monksway, had developed a keen interest in the breed and successfully imported Cobra von Boberstrand and Bando von Fohr into Britain in 1952. Interestingly, the first import from America, Heidi von Reiningen, arrived in the same year. She was in whelp at the time and her son, Thunderjet, was Best Dog at Crufts in 1955.

This is where the influence of American dogs in Britain began and continued through the lines from Valhalla's Helmsman Arrow, Flottheim's Kym, Kamsou Moonraker von Bismarck, Arimar's Rolf von der Reiteralm (longhair carrier), Am. Ch. Nani's Totally Awesome, and Am. Ch. Nani's Class Clown at Tasairgid, to name but a few. These all contributed to the Weimaraner population, producing Champions either directly or through the lines from Andelyb's A litter, Kympennas Tristan, Monroes Orest, Cartford (Cloud) litter, Smokey von Frambrue, Sandrock Coral, Wolfox Sandrock Cha-Cha, Strawbridge Madam, Lusco's Foreign Affair of FlimmoricRagstone Ryuhlan, Flimmoric Fanclub and Gunalt Tea Party as well as many others.

American breeding has influenced British conformation and temperament since 1952, and, as a result, Champions with American breeding outnumber those without by more than 4:1.

But let us take a closer look at those early British dogs. Having been so pleased with his first two imports, Major Petty went on to import six more, although he considered only three to be worthy of Kennel Club registration. Major Richardson brought in five more, and, again, only two were registered.

The 'blue' Weimaraner was a subject of major controversy in America.

Meanwhile, Mrs Olga Mallett imported a dog, Arco von der Kolfuster Heidi, and Babette von der Katzbach, who was already in whelp. The foundation and development of Weimaraners in Britain lay with these nine dogs together with Heidi von Reiningen from the United States.

In 1953, only one year after Weimaraners had set foot in the United Kingdom, the Weimaraner Club of Great Britain was formed with Major Petty as secretary. Gradually, numbers grew and there are three other clubs – the Weimaraner Association, the North of England Weimaraner Society and the Weimaraner Club of Scotland – all with Championship status.

Am. Ch. Nani's Class Clown at Tasairgid, imported from the USA.

LONGHAIRED WEIMARANERS

We must not ignore the early longhaired Weimaraners in Britain. First we should remember when the first longhair was shown in Germany. This was at the Hanover show of 1879. However, the first longhaired puppy to be 'recognised' was whelped in 1933 in Austria by Josef Schaffer out of two shorthaired parents.

Schaffer may have 'recognised' that the puppy was a longhair, but he sold it as a shorthair – but a bit 'fluffy'. He assured Robert Pattay, the puppy's new owner, that the 'fluffiness' would fall out! It didn't, of course, but undeterred Mr Pattay showed the pup, Tell von Stranzendorf, in Vienna in 1934. There was a great deal of interest and fascination from those present, among whom

was Major Herber, a renowned authority on the breed. After much research into the puppy's pedigree, he concluded that the coat variant was a natural part of the breed. He then consulted with the German Weimaraner Club. After long deliberation, the longhair variety was officially recognised in 1935.

In 1974, Ann Janson, having seen photographs of longhaired Weimaraners taken at the World Show in Czechoslovakia, imported Asta von gut Blaustauden. Later that year, she also imported Dino von der Hagardburg, again from Austria.

In Britain, a longhaired bitch, Pia aus der Greifenburg, made a short stop in England in 1972 en route for New Zealand from Germany. She was accompanied

by Arno von Hohenwald, a shorthaired dog with longhaired ancestors. Although registered with the Kennel Club, they were not bred from in Britain.

In addition, at least one longhaired Weimaraner had already been produced in a litter in Scotland in January 1973. This litter was bred by Mr I. Seymour and was sired by Ortega Opal Mint out of Grey Moonshadow of Duenna – both shorthairs and both carrying longhair genes. The surviving dog puppy went to Joan Matuszewska and was registered as Mafia Man of Monroes. After detailed research, it was found that, in order to find longhaired Weimaraners in the pedigree, it was necessary to go back at least six generations.

Sh. Ch. Pondridge Practical Joker: The UK's first longhaired Champion.

In 1975, the first all longhair litter was born out of Asta von gut Blaustauden by Dino von der Hagardburg. Negotiations to amend the Breed Standard to include longhairs were started between the Weimaraner Club of Great Britain and the Kennel Club. Final approval was given on 2 June 1976, but longhairs had to compete against shorthairs. The longhair variant was officially recognised, although they have not escalated in numbers over the years.

In 1981, the longhaired Pondridge Practical Joker was born. He was bred by Gill and Leo Smith out of Aruni Danya from Seicer and sired by the Smiths' Austrian import Hasso von der Hagardburg. In 1991, aged 10, he gained his Show Champion title. It had taken almost 20 years for the first Show Champion longhair to emerge from the first imports.

OUT OF BRITAIN AND AMERICA TO AUSTRALIA

Strawbridge Furst and Strawbridge Fidget, sired by the American-bred Thunderjet out of Major Petty's German import Cobra von Boberstrand, were sent to Australia in 1955. With these two went Strawbridge Graf and Strawbridge Gypsy, who were sired by Bando von Fohr out of Hella aus der Helmeude, giving a spread of breeding potential.

A little later, an American dog, Regal Wunder Columbian Duke, also arrived in Australia in 1959. This dog was brought in as a pet and sired only one litter before being tragically killed on the road.

In 1966, an American student moved to Australia with his pet Weimaraner, Fritz von Singen. The dog sired several litters, mainly to an imported British bitch called Halsall Brown Pheasant. She brought the working ability of her sire, Ch.

Strawbridge Oliver, and the quality breeding of her dam, Sandrock Coral.

Between the mid 1970s and 1980s, some of the few German imports arrived, both long and shorthaired, with the shorthaired dog Arno von Hoenwald and the longhaired bitch Pia aus der Greifenburg leading the way. One German dog, Salto von Zenthof, who was imported by John and Rosemary Mayhew, had spent some time in Britain, though he was not used extensively at stud.

The American dog, Sh. Ch. Arimar's Rolf von der Reiteralm, also spent some time in Britain where, out of several litters, he sired Ch. Reeman Aruac CDex, UDex, WDex, TDex. Arimar's Rolf was the next known dog to have been imported into Australia in 1981, again by the Mayhews. Sired by American Dual Champion Ronamax Rufus of Reiteralm CD out of Am. Ch. I've

THE WEIMARANER IN AUSTRALIA

Aust. Ch. Grauhund It'n'abit: Multiple Group winner.

Ch. Grauhund Nite Moves: This Weimaraner created breed history by winning Best in Show at the Sydney Royal Show 1993.

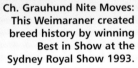

A Dream of Arimar CD, Arimar's Rolf brought versatility to the breed. He was an immediate success, winning his Australian Championship in a matter of weeks. His prowess at stud produced in the region of 61 Champions. The 1980s gave the genetic variation needed to develop a sound, even-tempered breed.

With the technology of artificial insemination and changes to the laws in Australia more semen was imported than actual dogs, giving breeders a greater degree of choice worldwide in both shorthaired and longhaired lines. Generally speaking, most imported semen came from American-bred dogs, including Am. Ch. Nani's Class Clown of

Tasairgid, sire of Am. Ch. Nani's Knocker CDX, TD, JH, NA, SD, VX, BROM, CGC, TT, TDI, the most qualified and versatile bitch of her time. 'Class' was imported into Scotland by Jean and Allan Fairlie. Frozen semen was sent to the Mayhews and his first 'mating' by A.I. produced a whole litter of Australian Champions. Lightly used at stud in the UK, he

Sh. Ch. Monroes Nexus: The first Weimaraner to win Best in Show at an Open Show.

is the sire of Sh. Ch. Gunalt Subject, runner-up Top Brood Bitch all breeds in 2002 and Sh. Ch. Gunalt First Class for Mianja still going strong in Veteran classes at the age of 11.

Australian Weimaraners have a wealth of quality, soundness and good temperaments thanks to the ingenuity and diversity of the breeders.

TOP BREEDERS, TOP DOGS

The story of the shorthaired Weimaraner is completely different from that of the longhaired. Major Petty's Strawbridge affix had a great influence on others, particularly the Sandrock affix owned by Mr and Mrs L.F. Causeley. Mr and Mrs Causeley's foundation bitch, Strawbridge Carol, was bred by Major Petty. Carol won four Best

of Breeds in a row at Crufts between 1955 through to 1958. She was the dam of Sandrock Admiral, owned by Dr Alex Mucklow. Admiral followed in her footsteps by winning Best of Breed at Crufts in 1959. Barbara Douglas-Redding also used Sandrock Admiral at stud, producing Sh. Ch. Ace of Acomb. This dog's ability to produce quality offspring also extended to siring Joan Matuszewska's (Monroes) first homebred Show Champion, Monroes Nexus and, in 1964, Sh. Ch. Monroes Nexus was the first Weimaraner to win Best in Show.

Championship status was granted by the Kennel Club in 1960 with four sets of Challenge Certificates – Crufts, Scottish Kennel Club (Glasgow), Blackpool and Birmingham. With

the increase in numbers, nowadays, all Championship shows have Challenge Certificates for the breed.

In that first year, 1960, at Blackpool, Mrs Barbara Douglas-Redding's bitch Wolfox Silverglance, incidentally sired by Sandrock Admiral, became the first female Show Champion and, at Birmingham, Strawbridge Oliver was crowned the first male Show Champion. In 1961, Show Champion Strawbridge Oliver qualified at the German Shorthaired Pointer Club field trials at Hailes Castle in Scotland to become the first full Champion in the breed.

In obedience, the first Obedience Challenge Certificate was awarded to Mrs Mary Milward's bitch, Strawbridge Irene, in 1958, later gaining

MAKING HISTORY

Weimaraner Association Championship Show 1998: Reserve Best in Show Mosey's Gunalt Dame of Denmo (left), handled by Patsy Hollings and Best in Show Ch. Kalimor Cooper, handled by Tina Morris.

The first Weimaraner Association Championship Show (pictured left to right): Stephen Hollings with Sh. Ch. Gunalt Obsession, Pauline Brooks with Sh. Ch. Amtrak Ameros at Ormerod, and Patsy Hollings with Gunalt Rover.

CDex (Companion Dog Excellent) in working trials. To date, there has not been an Obedience Champion in the breed in Britain. Perhaps it can be said that working trials and field trials are more suited to the Weimaraner instinct.

There have been numerous Champions who have qualified in the show ring, in field trials and also in working trials. They include: Ch. Fossana Bruno CDex, UDex, WDex, TD owned by Val O'Keefe; Ch. Monroes Ambition of Westglade CDex, UDex, WD owned by Gwen Sowersby; and Ch. Reeman Aruac CDex, UDex, WDex, Tdex, owned by Bob Lynch and the most qualified dog to date. But it took until 1988 before Ritisons Constellation CDex, UDex, WDex, TDex, owned by Jenny Wilson, became the first Working Trial Champion in the breed in Britain.

In Britain when field trials for Hunt, Point, Retrieve breeds are run, all HPR breeds compete together. There are, of course, different styles among the differing breeds, so it is no wonder that there has only been one male Field Trial Champion – FT CH Wobrooke of Fleetapple owned by Di Arrowsmith. In 2005, Quadet Caterin, owned by Dave Pilkington, gained her Field Trial Championship.

THE GUNALT STORY

Drive along a country lane in Yorkshire, England, and you are greeted by a veritable feast of Weimaraners – dogs and bitches alike, all running together, tails wagging, eager to see the visitors. You have arrived at the home of Patsy and Stephen Hollings of Gunalt Weimaraners – top breeders all breeds 14 times, top breeders in Weimaraners 19 times, breeders of the breed Challenge Certificate record holder Sh. Ch. Gunalt Harris Tweed who, in turn, sired the bitch Challenge Certificate record holder Sh. Ch. Ansona Purdy.

Patsy and Stephen are holders of the Tom Horner Award of Excellence for 2005 awarded at the Pup of the Year competition and the Pedigree Top Breeder award for 2005. These two awards are decided on by Dog World and Pedigree Masterfoods respectively for outstanding contribution to dogs.

To give some idea of that contribution to Weimaraners, Patsy and Stephen have owned and/or bred 62 Champions in Weimaraners, Champion English Setters and Hungarian Vizslas with Reserve CCs in Field Spaniels and Golden Retrievers. Add to that impressive record 13 individual Gundog Group winners and 18 Group 2s, with Gunalt Joy winning Top Brood Bitch, all breeds, in 1995 and runner-up in 1994 and 1996.

Sh. Ch. Gunalt Subject was sired by Am. Ch. Nani's Class Clown of Tasairgid (USA Imp) out of

Ir. Sh. & Sh. Ch. Gunalt Harris Tweed: Breed record holder, owned by Karen Robinson.

Sh. Ch. Gunalt First Class, sister to Gunalt Subject. Owned by Mary Waite and handled by Jackie Ward

Group winner Sh. Ch. Gunalt Tea Party. Subject was not shown until she was 14 months, when she won the Challenge Certificate and Best of Breed. She was also runner-up Top Brood Bitch, all breeds, in 2002. It is interesting to note that many of the Show Champion Weimaraners were owned and handled by newcomers to the breed not just in Britain but also in South Africa, Australia, New Zealand and Barbados. Not a bad record, and all since 1976.

Sh. Ch. Gunalt Intuition: Winning the Gundog Group at Paignton Championship Show.

Sh. Ch. Gunalt Obsession: This big-winning sister to Harris Tweed won 30CCs and 5 Groups, as well as taking Best Bitch in Show at Birmingham Championship Show.

FIELD TRIAL CH. QUADET CATERIN

It was back in 1986 when David Pilkington first became involved with Weimaraners, having had two companions with a bit of working flair. In 1999, following some research into good working bloodlines, David was told of a litter of newborn Weimaraners in Dorset, bred by Steve and Marilyn Chant out of Quadet Asta and sired by Brakabreeze Goshawk. Dave purchased a female, and Quadet Caterin joined his household.

As a puppy, Quadet Caterin (Holly) was very biddable, enthusiastic and confident in any situation, and the close bond that is essential to create a good foundation for basic training was quickly formed. She did well in gundog working tests through all classes from Puppy through to Open, achieving awards along the way. At the Weimaraner Club of Great Britain's 50th Anniversary Weekend, she was given high marks for her working capabilities and she was awarded first place in the Open Class of the club's Gundog Working Test.

From the shooting season of 2002, David started to enter Holly in field trials. On her first trip out, she gained a third place in Novice, the only award given on the day. In January 2005, at the age of five years and after gaining numerous field trial awards, Holly had gained her second 'first place' in an Open Class trial. This gave her the title of Field Trial Champion – she was the first Weimaraner bitch to receive the title in the history of the breed in the country.

The Pilkingtons now have a new addition, having imported Reha (Woksebs Reha Swe Imp), a Weimaraner bitch bred in Sweden by Anders and Elisabeth Beskow using their bitch Swe. Ch. Woksebs Nike and the sire from Germany, Ansum Von Reersom. Reha comes from good working lines, which could prove a valuable contribution for the future of the working Weimaraner in Great Britain.

Field Trial Champion Quadet Caterin: The first Weimaraner bitch to be awarded this title.

The number of Dual Champions and Field Champions in America runs into hundreds and there are, in Britain, numerous full Champions – dogs who have become Show Champions and have also won a qualifying place in a field trial. But it is disappointing that there remain just the two British Field Trial Champions.

The history of the Weimaraner in Britain could not be complete without mention of Sh. Ch. Flimmoric Fanclub, sired by American Champion Nani's Totally Awesome out of American import Lusco's Foreign Affair of Flimmoric. Awesome was quarantined in Britain when *en route* for Australia and only sired this one litter before heading off for pastures new. Fanclub brought substance, conformation and an exceptional temperament to the breed. There are few pedigrees of quality dogs in which he does not feature. He is the breed's all-time top stud dog, siring more than 20 Champions.

CONCLUSION

Through the 1970s to the 1990s, on both sides of the Atlantic, the popularity of the breed has increased dramatically – to fourth most popular in American registrations and tenth in Britain. Breeding for quantity became almost the norm. New owners attracted to the breed by media attention soon realised that the Weimaraner has special needs that they could not, or would not, provide – companionship, training, socialisation, leadership and respect.

This popularity explosion had created quantity breeding by puppy farmers with no regard to quality, either in health or temperament. Exposure on television had drawn the attention of the public. Unable to acquire a well-bred puppy from a responsible breeder and being unwilling to wait, would-be owners had turned to the puppy farmers, often with dire consequences – such as illness, even death and, more often than not, questionable temperaments. After all the careful planning of dedicated breeders, the damage was done. Still, to this day, the breed rescue organisations are inundated with Weimaraners needing new homes.

However, following on from those early proponents of the breed, the commitment to selection for quality and sound temperaments will continue and the Weimaraner will remain that most special of breeds.

END NOTES

1 As shown in the Pierpont Morgan Library, New York City

2 August Stroese, Unser Hund Neumann 1902 quoted in Denlinger Weimaraner 25

3 Robert a. d. Herber, Deutsche Waidwerk 22 Sep. 1939 quoted in Denlinger Weimaraner 26,28

4 Denlinger Weimaraner 25. This passage is quoted in many archives but original source remains unidentified.

5 Beckmann Geschichte 1:169

A WEIMARANER FOR YOUR LIFESTYLE

Chapter 3

You have decided it is time for a new addition to the family in the form of a puppy. As with meeting a life partner, physical attraction is what initially draws you to a breed. The advantage of choosing a pedigree dog over a mixed breed mongrel is that you can find out about a breed, both in terms of appearance and temperament, so you can discover if it is the right breed to suit your lifestyle. There is nothing wrong with opting for a mongrel, but it is much more of a blind learning experience, as you have very little idea as to how an individual dog will turn out.

Buying a puppy should be regarded as taking on a new member of the family – it is nothing like setting out to buy a new car! The Weimaraner is a beautiful dog, with a unique colour, and appears easy to look

after. The dog has class; he is aristocratic in looks and gives the impression that the owner of such a breed is high on the social scale. An excellent reason to buy a car – not a good reason to buy a dog! The rehoming charity campaign that states: "A dog is not just for Christmas" is 100 per cent relevant; a responsible owner will realise that the commitment of a dog is with you all the year round, and for 12 years or more.

Your Weimaraner will be what you make of him, providing you have a well-bred dog that is typical of the breed. Each pedigree breed is bred to fulfil a specific purpose. A retriever will carry slippers about, as his job is to bring back your dinner when shot. A setter will rush off when released from his lead, in effect to 'set' the potential game. The Weimaraner is a hunt, point, retrieve breed, German in origin,

bred to hunt through the thick forests of Weimar. Game would have included wild boar, which is both agile and dangerous. Therefore, the Weimaraner must be quick thinking, able to assess what is before him; he should hold his game at bay until his master comes to deal with it, protect himself from foe, or, indeed, protect his master from the ravages of the ferocious boar. The result is a lot of dog, with a strong German disposition, who is capable of protecting, yet with a sensible, gentle temperament.

To be compatible with a Weimaraner you need to be quietly determined, more stubborn than your charge, and black and white in commands. I would sum up the Weimaraner with the phrase: "The Weimaraner does not suffer fools gladly". This is an intelligent dog, questioning, courageous, powerful, extremely stubborn,

This is a highly intelligent breed that does not suffer fools gladly.

sensitive, protective and biddable. You do not get 'owt for nowt', as we say in Yorkshire. In fact, the best and most fulfilling achievements are those we work hard for, be it a happy, secure family or a well-reared pet. Therefore, the groundwork is essential.

It is easy to find a Weimaraner puppy for sale advertised in the local paper, but act in haste and repent at leisure. The size, protective instinct and light eye suggest to some misguided folk that the Weimaraner would make a guard dog. This is not the case. The Weimaraner is a dog who likes to be with people, not left to prowl a compound. I am not sure that dogs of any breed should be exploited in this way,

but it is certainly not the lifestyle for a Weimaraner.

WEIMARANERS AND CHILDREN

People ring me to ask if a Weimaraner is likely to be good with children. This is a logical question, as most people think about buying a dog when the partner has left work in order to look after children, or when children have started school and free time has become available to devote to puppy training and rearing. In these situations, yes, a Weimaraner gets on well with children. If, on the other hand, the enquiries come from people who want a Weimaraner to amuse and occupy the children while they do something else, the

answer is no.

Weimaraners are gundogs. The reason why gundogs make ideal family pets is because they are soft mouthed. This means that, if the adrenaline is flowing due to playing hard with you or your children, the dog resorts to instinct. The gundog's natural instinct is to retrieve dead game with due care so that it remains intact and is therefore fit to eat. Translating this to a domestic situation, a gundog acting on instinct is less likely to snap or bite.

Although the Weimaraner makes a wonderful family pet, he is too headstrong and powerful to be left in sole control of a child. This is a mentally strong dog who will become wilful and disobedient if he is reared without authority. Therefore, a young child, who does not have authority, will struggle to impose a sense of leadership and you will end up with a badly behaved dog. A Weimaraner has questioning intelligence and needs mental stimulation. He can find children boring and lose interest in them very quickly. When my children were small, they played happily, leading a setter around the garden for hours. The Weimaraner would only tolerate this for a short period of time and would leave the children in the lurch when he had had enough. The same things now happen with my grandson.

No matter how trustworthy your Weimaraner appears to be, he should never be left unattended with children. I had a call from a distressed owner to say the family dog had nipped a child from next door, who had come round to play with their children. When I enquired as to the circumstances, I was informed that the mother had gone out to put washing on the line and left the children playing in the house completely unsupervised. She had no knowledge of the circumstances that initiated the fracas, yet immediately presumed the dog had wandered over and snapped at the child, which is highly unlikely. Children often scream and play fight in excitement: how is a dog to know this is not for real? In this situation a Weimaraner cannot be blamed

for trying to protect his family. A little forethought – not leaving young children on their own with the dog – would have prevented the incident. I would ask that mother, would you leave the children playing near a carving knife or unguarded fire?

In fact, a child under the age of 16 should never be allowed to take a dog out for a walk unattended, whatever the breed. A child with a Cocker Spaniel could quite happily go to play in a park, but who knows what irresponsible owner, with a large unruly dog, may also be at the park? How would a young child cope if their dog were suddenly attacked?

All too often, dogs are taken for rehoming because the family is expecting a new baby. There is

absolutely no need for this, as long as care is taken. The Weimaraner is a devoted and possessive dog and will feel jealous of the love and attention the newcomer receives. However, this can be balanced by giving your Weimaraner quality time so that he does not feel ignored. It is also important that your Weimaraner learns to accept short periods on his own so that you can give your full attention to the baby when required. Ideally, your Weimaraner should be happy to settle in his indoor crate at times when you cannot supervise him.

WORK SCHEDULE
If all occupants of the home work a 9-5 day, with the children out at school, you must weigh up

The Weimaraner interacts well with children but will look to an adult for leadership.

A Weimaraner will tolerate limited time on his own, but this is a dog that thrives on human company.

possessions. Before embarking on dog ownership, it is worth trying to plan ahead. Where will you be in five years' time? If one partner is at home, perhaps looking after small children now, they may wish to return to work at a later day. Your responsibility to your dog is virtually as great as that to your children. It is not fair to expect a dog that has had your undivided attention to be left for long periods on a regular basis. The rules you begin with are those that your Weimaraner understands. So if you envisage a change of circumstances at a future date, it may be a good idea to provide an outside kennel or run or an indoor kennel/crate so that your Weimaraner learns to accept periods on his own right from the start.

It is also worth investigating dog walking/pet sitting options that are available, so that your Weimaraner does not have to spend the day on his own. However, think long and hard about the dangers of allowing your Weimaraner to be exercised by someone else. It is a great responsibility to look after someone else's dog. Nine times out of ten, the walker will be able to let the dog off the lead in a safe area with no problems, but you just need one time for the dog to be distracted by a rabbit scurrying out of the hedge, for instance, and the dog can be gone.

A number of kennels also provide day care facilities, where you can drop off your dog in the morning and collect him after

whether you can give a dog a good quality of life, or if you would be better suited to the more independent lifestyle of a cat. No dog, least of all a Weimaraner, can cope with a quick walk to the park five nights a week and then a hike over the mountains on Saturday and Sunday. This is not a dog who will sit happily, hour after hour, chewing a bone while you are at work. The Weimaraner never does anything absentmindedly; he will first work out why and if. Consequently, the dog who decides to chew can easily go through a door or take the plaster off a wall, and it is not unheard of for a Weimaraner to destroy a settee. Conversely, if a Weimaraner is stimulated and occupied, he should never chew anything other than his own

It is a bonus if you can take your Weimaraner on holiday, but if this is not possible, you will have to make suitable arrangements.

work. This is as acceptable as nursery care for your children. In fact, it can be beneficial, as your growing young dog will learn different disciplines and social skills, rather like a child, which can be of benefit.

HOLIDAYS
Holidays need to be planned, or at least discussed, about before taking on a Weimaraner. Decisions need to be made as to whether you are happy to board your Weimaraner in kennels, or whether you'd prefer to use a home sitting service. As the owner of boarding kennels for over 28 years, I understand that leaving your pet is like leaving your child with a stranger – after all, your pet is a member of the family. However, it is not realistic

to dismiss the idea of boarding kennels in the hope that a family member will be available to take care of your dog. No matter what the good intentions, outside circumstances may mean that this is not a practical solution.

The Weimaraner is very people orientated and can become stressed when separated from his owner, especially in a kennel environment. However, if the dog is boarded from a young age and learns to enjoy playing with members of staff and other friendly dogs, he will form a good association with the kennel environment. It is therefore wise to leave your Weimaraner for short periods – perhaps just a weekend or two – before he is 18 months old.

We once boarded a five-year-

old Weimaraner who had been indulged by his owners for all his life. His world ended during his two-week stay, and despite feeding him everything and anything, he lost weight very quickly, as Weimaraners are prone to do. No doubt his owners thought we had neglected him. Little did they realise that it was their 'kindness' that had caused his distress. Lots of breeds react differently in boarding kennels; some breeds sit and sulk, but eat heartily and go home looking wonderful. This is certainly not the case with a Weimaraner. A Weimaraner that is accustomed to boarding kennels from an early age will generally have a whale of a time. He will eat if fed correctly, enjoy his walks and play times, but he

There can be unforeseen expense involved in owning a dog.

may still lose weight. He may even get a tummy upset on returning home, brought on by the excitement of being reunited with his owners. So don't be alarmed if your dog has lost weight after a spell in kennels. Simply feed light meals for a day or so until his digestion returns to normal and his stress levels subside.

It is a good idea to provide your dog with an old towel or blanket that smells of home, so he doesn't feel totally deserted. Remember, though: the kennels will have lots of bedding to wash and as your comfort blanket will probably need laundering during his stay, it could become lost, so don't take his favourite bedding.

It is also possible to have a home sitter to look after your dog when you are on holiday. This enables your pet to stay in his own surroundings, and it also provides added security for your home. This will probably entail more expense than boarding your dog, and you will have a stranger in your home. Checking credentials is therefore essential, as is providing a detailed account so the home sitter will be able to implement a daily routine to suit your dog's needs.

YOUR AGE

This consideration may seem a strange one – yet think about it. If you had a puppy when you were 30, and he lived for 12 years, you would quickly forget the first two years of his life. You would look back at the cute puppy photos and fail to remember all the hard work: the house training, learning social skills within the home, the initial sleepless nights, and, of course, those dreadful adolescent months. The next 10 years blend into an idyllic dream, followed by the heartbreaking trauma of losing a beloved pet.

Taking on a new puppy in middle age can be a whole new ball game. How many times do we hear the cry: "He's not like Rosie was"? Your circumstances have, no doubt, changed, and it is all too easy to forget the testing times when your first dog was growing up. On the other hand, you may find you have more patience, more free time and more motivation, all of which will be ideal for a Weimaraner – and owning such an active dog will certainly save you much money on gym membership!

COST

An important point to consider is whether you can afford to care for a dog for the duration of his life. When people ring me to enquire about Weimaraners, I am filled with trepidation if the first question is, "How much are they?" The initial cost of the pup is not the final figure, nor is it what owning a Weimaraner is all about. You have to consider the costs incurred throughout a dog's life, which include: price, habitat, food, medical expenses, boarding fees… the list is quite endless.

Just as if you were starting a family, unforeseen costs are always arising. The smart coupé may be a prized possession, but an expensive estate car is more practical following the addition of a large Weimaraner. Once the estate car is obtained, it should be fitted with a dog guard. The clever Weimaraner soon fathoms how to knock down a cheap dog guard or how to squeeze through it. This is not only annoying but dangerous, as a Weimaraner usually performs this while the driver is the sole occupant and is trying to concentrate on driving the car. The solution is an expensive dog guard or dog crate.

Veterinary costs should also be considered. Although the

Both the female (left) and the male (right) are loving and loyal.

Weimaraner is generally a healthy breed, you will still need to cover initial costs of vaccinations and worming. Most people insure against veterinary fees and death, but insurance can be expensive.

In terms of general care, you will need to provide suitable accommodation, such as an indoor kennel or a dog basket, plus bedding (see Chapter Four: The New Arrival). Feeding costs can make a big hole in the budget, and you will also need to budget for kennelling fees when you go on holiday, or day care services if you work.

GREAT EXPECTATIONS

Before you go out and buy a Weimaraner, you should decide exactly what you want from your dog, and this will help you to make the right choice.

MALE OR FEMALE?

Choosing whether to buy a dog or a bitch is purely a matter of personal preference. I have lost count of the times I have heard people say that a bitch is more loving than a dog, only equalled by the number of people who say that a dog is more loyal. In fact, both sexes are loving and loyal.

HUNT, POINT, RETRIEVE BREEDS

The all-purpose gundogs that can carry out all facets of work in the field.

Italian Spinone.

German Shorthaired Pointer.

Without wishing to humanise dogs, the difference is best explained by saying that a female Weimaraner tends to be rather like a woman. She tends to be more manipulative, and she thinks about what she's going to get out of doing as she is told. She is very sweet when it suits her, and rather aloof when it doesn't.

A bitch usually comes into heat or season every six months, and this lasts for three weeks. If the bitch is not neutered, you may have your work cut out keeping her away from interested males at this time. She may also suffer a false pregnancy, and resulting

behaviour can range from being quiet and broody, to making beds, digging up the garden and confiscating children's toys. Some bitches produce milk and even go off their food. We find that some of our bitches become quick tempered with their peers a week or two before coming into season. However, in general, a female Weimaraner is gentle, loving and pleasant to live with.

A male Weimaraner tends to be more even-tempered than a female. He may be very loyal, but only if he respects his owner. I have often found that a male is more patient with children, in the same way that a father can be.

However, it is important to bear in mind that a male is two inches (5 cms) bigger than the female, and this does not just mean taller. To be balanced, the male is bigger overall and more powerful. In adolescence, he can become very much like a teenager: hot-headed and physical. Because of his strength and power, this can unnerve someone who is not familiar with the breed. A first-time owner may well need support and help from the breeder or an experienced Weimaraner owner at this time.

Weimaraners are a protective breed, and the male Weimaraner may see himself as pack leader –

Hungarian Vizsla.

The enquiring mind of the Weimaraner is ideally suited to the challenging work he is required to do. *David Tomlinson*

needing to look after his family – if he is not taught his place in the pecking order from the onset (see Chapter Six: Training and Socialisation).

COAT TYPE

One of the visual appeals of the Weimaraner is his sleek, athletic appearance. Weimaraners do moult, but they have no undercoat and so are naturally clean, with mud and dirt falling away from the coat readily. White hair is the coarsest type, so the soft, grey hair of this breed is less likely to stick to clothes or to show on furniture. You tend to think the kitchen floor looks

clean – until you brush it and find all the debris gathered in the dustpan!

The longhaired variety is not as prolific in numbers or as popular as the smooth-haired Weimaraner. Personally, I feel that this is because one loses the streamline effect with the longhaired type, and yet the coat is not long and glamorous, as it is in the Afghan Hound or setter breeds, for example.

I find that the longhaireds have a slightly different temperament: they tend to be more 'birdy', meaning a longhaired Weimaraner is much more interested in watching birds fly

and air scenting than the shorthairs. My theory, and it is not substantiated, is that many years ago someone wanted to speed up the scenting activity of the breed, which in the shorts can be slower and ground scenting in style, possibly from some hound origin. It is possible that setters were introduced into the breeding programme and, just maybe, that is where the longcoat variety emerged.

CHOOSING A ROLE

The Weimaraner excels as a working gundog, a show dog, and a companion dog, but it is best to decide what you want

If you want to exhibit your Weimaraner in the ring, you will need to go to a breeder that specialises in show lines.

from your Weimaraner in advance so you can find a breeder who specialises in producing the type you want. When you have made your decision, you may need to be prepared to wait for a suitable puppy. If you want a nice, sound puppy as a pet, you may not have to wait too long, but you may need to be patient if you want a dog with show or working potential. Remember, it will not cost you any more to buy a well-bred, typical puppy than it would for a badly bred, unsound or untypical specimen, so take your time and make sure you get what you want.

WORKING GUNDOG
The Weimaraner is one of seven breeds classified under the heading Hunt, Point, Retrieve, or HPR as we label them. The other breeds within this group are: the Brittany, the German Shorthaired Pointer (GSP), the German Wirehaired Pointer (GWP), the Hungarian Vizsla, the Italian Spinone, and the Large Munsterlander.

The HPR breeds lend themselves to different working facets in the field. A HPR dog is a 'jack of all trades' and needs an enquiring mind to cope with the different work requirements. This is exactly what the Weimaraner

has, which is why he would not make a good couch potato. In all gundogs the original instinct can be noted at some point; even show types display their inherent instinct to some degree. The Golden Retriever always wants to carry something, the Irish Setter ranges the park at great speed, the Cocker Spaniel merrily works through the undergrowth – yet many gundog breeds, including the aforementioned, have split into two totally different types – working or show.

It is generally accepted that the HPR breeds shown in the ring are more likely to have retained their working instinct, good conformation and temperament than the other gundog breeds. Years ago, many of the older gundog breeds living in the UK were bred for working and showing abilities, which served to split the breeds into differing types. Today, working setters, spaniels and retrievers are very different to the strains of these breeds that we are used to seeing in the show ring. Latterly it was realised that this was not good for the future of pedigree breeds of dogs; health, conformation, type and working ability should be retained at all costs. With these points in mind, and with the guidance of the forward thinking Kennel Club, it became evident that breeders should preserve all attributes pertaining to the blueprint of breeds. Consequently, breeds that came into the country in the middle of the 20th century had the advantage of more enlightened breeders.

The breeder will help you to evaluate whether a puppy has show potential.
lynn@kipps.co.uk

You can work your Weimaraner without actually going out with a gun and shooting over him. Decide what work you intend to do with your dog before embarking on a search for a breeder.

COMPANION

A Weimaraner for a companion is a priority not only for you but for the dog himself. A much-loved Weimaraner that is given plenty of stimulation and the required amount of care, attention and exercise will be as much a companion to you as a show or working dog. In all instances, the Weimaraner will not respond to you unless the elements of care and responsibility are fulfilled.

You may wish to give a home to an older Weimaraner rather than a buying a puppy. However, rehoming an adult does not simply mean that you are missing out on the hard work of rearing a puppy. An older dog may be set in his ways, and you may well find that it takes both time and patience to help him settle. The older the dog, the more set in his ways he will be. For instance, chewing in a puppy is one thing, but an adult dog can be highly destructive. Defiance in a puppy can easily be rectified; in a two-year-old it can be very unnerving. If you want to give a caring, loving home to an older dog in need, think very carefully, making sure you have removed the rose-coloured spectacles.

SHOW DOG

No breeder with any experience will claim to sell a 'definite show puppy'. I always say: "I do not have a crystal ball" – foreseeing the future is for people with greater powers than I possess. So much can change as a puppy grows up, and, to a great extent, that is what is so fascinating about showing and breeding dogs. However, selecting a reputable breeder is the best and only way forward if you want a Weimaraner with show potential.

FINDING A BREEDER

Where do you find a reputable breeder once you have decided what you want from your Weimaraner? The Kennel Club, which is easily accessible via the internet and the telephone, is a great starting point. The Kennel Club works diligently for the good of dogs and promotes and helps breeders in their quest to

There is nothing more appealing than a Weimaraner puppy, but you must think long and hard before taking on the commitment.

lynn@kipps.co.uk

breed healthy, sound litters. The Kennel Club has introduced an accredited breeders scheme, and breeders have to fulfil certain criteria in order to achieve this status. The Kennel Club has a representative who visits kennels owned by members of this scheme to ensure good practice is maintained in accordance with guidelines issued. Therefore, it is worth taking advantage of breeders who are members of this scheme.

When people express an interest in a Weimaraner, we often invite them to visit our kennels, have a coffee, watch the dogs, ask questions and find out about the breed. Folk often take us up on this offer from all over the country. They go home, think about what they have seen and heard in the cold light of day, and then make a decision as to whether this is the breed for them. Once that decision is made, those people make fine owners. It is the people who find a half-hour journey too far, unless you have puppies available, that worry me.

Research is invaluable. The Kennel Club will put you in touch with individual breed clubs. These clubs often have websites, giving valuable advice and information about the breed, and also what questions to ask a breeder before visiting the kennels. An established breeder will have an affix. This is rather like a trade name and all dogs bred by that kennel bear the affix. For instances, my affix is Gunalt. The point of an affix is that breeders can identify specific dogs, and different lines can be traced when looking at pedigrees. From the buyer's point of view, you can easily research affixes in the dog press, as the names of winning dogs will often appear there.

WHAT TO EXPECT FROM A BREEDER

When you have decided on the Weimaraner and the 'line' that is most suitable, you will then have to be patient until a litter of puppies is available. When you ring up about a particular litter, do not be afraid to ask questions. A reputable breeder will be happy to answer numerous questions to ensure that their puppies go to the right homes. A few examples of questions you may wish to ask are:

- Are the puppies Kennel Club registered and with a full pedigree?
- How old are the puppies?
- How many puppies are in the litter?
- How many litters has the dam of this litter had?
- Can both parents be seen?
- Have both parents had all health check requirements and recommendations for their particular breed?
- Have the puppies been wormed regularly?
- Have the puppies been vaccinated?
- Does the breeder give a diet sheet and after-care information with each puppy for sale?

When you are satisfied that you have the right answers to these questions, you may wish to

HEALTH CHECK

Health issues are of paramount importance and all breeding stock should have the health clearances required for the breed. With Weimaraners, all breeding stock should be X-rayed for hip dysplasia, commonly known as HD. The lower the score, the better the hip placement in the socket; the breed average for Weimaraners is around 15.

The Weimaraner does not tend to suffer major problems with hips, as puppies are not too heavy, which can put pressure on the joints, resulting in growth problems.

make an appointment to view the puppies for sale.

If the person you are dealing with tells you that there are no papers with the litter of puppies for sale, or that the relevant papers will be sent on to you, do not fall for it. Kennel Club registrations take a maximum of 10 days to be processed, and reputable breeders will ensure that they have sent for these documents in plenty of time before their puppies are due to be sold.

When you go to view the litter, check that all the puppies appear healthy and alert, and that they are living in a clean, warm environment. Do ask to look at the dam and the sire of the puppies if possible. The stud dog may not live at the home of

the puppies and mother, as a good breeder will use a stud who is compatible to the dam's breeding lines, which will probably mean the breeder has to travel great distances to use the 'right' stud dog. However, if you have researched your breed well and found a long-established breeder with a sound reputation, you should be able to see dogs of different generations, which will also give you an insight into the temperament that the puppy will have inherited.

CHOOSING A PUPPY

How do you choose a puppy from the litter? The old ethos is: don't pick the puppy who sits in the corner. The theory behind this is that you do not want a nervous or shy puppy. This dog could react physically to unexpected actions or noises, which could result in a threat to people, such as a snap at a running child, or being aggressive with another dog. However, this type of temperament is unlikely to be seen if you go to an established breeder who has a passion for the breed. Through years of experience and careful breeding for soundness and good temperament, this type of breeder will be able to advise

You are looking for an evenly matched litter where all the puppies are clean and appear lively and healthy.

How do you decide which puppy is most likely to suit your lifestyle?

COAT TYPES

The shorthaired Weimaraner is a more popular choice, but the longhaired Weimaraner has a special appeal.

and help you to choose a puppy. A breeder knows the pedigree intimately and will know which puppy is likely to fit in with a particular family's lifestyle. As with siblings, human or canine, each will have slightly different personalities. The message here is always work with the breeder, for whom the puppies' welfare is paramount. You will often be encouraged to visit puppies during their first weeks of life.

THE FINAL DECISION
It is important that you never feel pressurised into purchasing a puppy. Taking on a Weimaraner is a hugely important decision, and one you will live with for the next 12 years or more. It is also important that you feel able to call on the breeder for help and advice throughout your Weimaraner's life.

THE NEW ARRIVAL

Chapter 4

Now you have chosen your Weimaraner puppy, you will have to wait until he is old enough to leave his mother and his littermates and is ready to move to his new home. While you are waiting for the big day, there are important preparations to be made.

IN THE HOUSE

One of the first decisions to make is where you want your puppy to sleep. You may think it is better if he is close to you, i.e. in the bedroom, but be aware that what you start with will be difficult to alter. So if your long-term aim is for your Weimaraner to sleep in the kitchen or in a downstairs room, it is best to start as you mean to go on. If you try to change locations, the puppy may lose the security of his initial familiar surroundings and

become noisy and disruptive.

Leaving your puppy with the freedom of the house could lead to disaster, as an inquisitive puppy will find mischief. At best, he will destroy your possessions; at worst he could injure himself by jumping up at surfaces and pulling utensils on him, chewing electric wires, or climbing up and down stairs and risking a fall.

IN THE GARDEN

The garden is a joyous place for a puppy, and many are expert gardeners, often removing the most expensive plants in favour of the most prolific weed! If you want to preserve your lawn, do not leave the puppy out to play for long periods unattended or he may dig.

The garden should be securely fenced, preferably so the puppy cannot see out, so he will have no need to run up and down, barking at passers-by. Likewise,

he will not get into the habit of enjoying a game with next door's dog, racing up and down and creating a muddy path. With regard to the height of the fencing, it should be between 5-6 ft (1.52-1.83 metres) so it is not inviting to jump. Remember, the grass is always greener on the other side.

Some plants are poisonous to dogs, so check with an expert at your garden centre, or do some research on the internet before you bring your puppy home. A garden pond can prove hazardous for an inquisitive puppy, so it is best to cover it or fence it off from the rest of the garden. Frogs live around ponds and are dangerous to dogs if they are picked up. The frog secretes poison, which can cause foaming at the mouth and send the dog into shock and collapse.

It is wise to check products used in the garden, such as weed

Puppies are great explorers, so you need to ensure that your garden is safe and secure.

killers and insecticides, which could be lethal if ingested. If you have used these products for years before you acquired a dog, you may not even realise the potential danger.

BUYING EQUIPMENT
There are now specialist 'supermarkets' that cater for all your dog's requisites. Vet centres also stock dog food, toys and leads, but are often more expensive and offer less choice.

INDOOR CRATE
An indoor crate/kennel is an invaluable purchase when rearing a puppy, and it will serve your Weimaraner well throughout his life. Obviously you have to make the initial investment, but this often works out cheaper than having to repair property that has been ruined by chewing or fouling.

The ideal size of crate for a female is: 36 x 23.5 x 26 inches (90 x 60 x 66 cms); a male needs a slightly bigger size: 41.5 x 28 x 30 inches (105 x 71 x 76 cms). It is best to purchase the adult size initially, which saves cost. An adult dog will use his crate only to sleep

in, so as long as the dog can stretch out, the crate does not need to be any bigger.

The crate is a great aid for house training (see page 62), and also benefits a puppy's development. If you have a baby, you will love it, nurture it, feed, cuddle and keep it clean and warm. You will also put the baby in his pram to rest and grow for much of the time. When a puppy is crate trained, he will be shut in to rest at times throughout the day. If the puppy is left to settle on a bed, he will be tempted to move when you get up to answer the phone, make a drink, or when the children come in, so he will not get the rest he needs. If the crate door is closed, he will get into the habit of settling from an early age, which benefits his development and stops him thinking he has to follow you wherever you go, even to the bathroom!

The crate is easily dismantled, so you can take it on holiday to a cottage, hotel or to a friend's home, where the dog will have his own safe environment. You are also secure in the knowledge that your dog cannot embarrass you by being destructive through the stress of being left in a strange place. The dog will not bark or worry, as he will settle in his own bed.

When you are travelling, it is safer for your dog to travel in a crate, and it gives you more flexibility. Your car will stay clean and, if you are out on a warm day, the windows and back door of the car can be left open in full knowledge that the dog is secure.

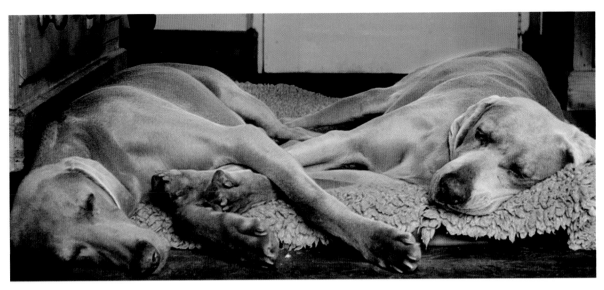

An adult will appreciate a comfortable place to sleep. *Photo courtsey: David Paige.*

In the awful event of an accident, a crate will stop the dog from escaping and possibly being run over.

BEDDING
The rubber-backed fleece bedding that is made specifically for dogs is perfect for putting in the crate for the dog to rest on. It is non-toxic, difficult to destroy by chewing, lets moisture through so the puppy is not lying in wet, and it is warm and easy to wash. If you buy two pieces, you can have a clean piece in the bed and the other in the wash, which is great while your puppy is being house trained.

DOG BED
You may wish to have a bed that your dog can use when not in his crate. Many different types are available. Moulded plastic beds are hygienic, and fleece bedding can be used to make them comfortable. Much more attractive is the woven basket, but a young dog can easily chew this, leaving sharp pieces of wicker that may be swallowed. The padded cloth beds come in cute designs but are hard to keep clean, as they are too big to fit in a washing machine. We have padded beds covered in heavy gauge synthetic material, which can be hosed down. We use a piece of fleece on these beds, which is washed regularly to avoid it smelling. What would we do without fleece bedding for dogs?

FOOD AND WATER BOWLS
Because Weimaraners are determined creatures, it is best to invest in stainless-steel bowls from the start. I have heard of a Weimaraner trying to chew an aluminium bowl, and he needed surgery to remove it from his teeth. Plastic dishes are often chewed and eaten. Again, these can cause problems to the digestive system. Ceramic dishes are often carried about by Weimaraners as a party trick, or when the dog decides it is teatime, and then dropped at your feet, shattering in pieces.

STORAGE BINS
It is obviously cheaper, when feeding a large breed such as a Weimaraner, to buy food in bulk. Storage must be thought of and a plastic dustbin can be a good idea. This will keep vermin out and keep the food dry. Do not leave it in a place accessible to

your Weimaraner, as they are extremely clever at getting in feed containers or, indeed, fridges. Most Weimaraner owners will be able to tell you where to buy a fridge lock!

GROOMING GEAR
Weimaraners do not need a huge amount of grooming equipment. It is better to buy a small number of high-quality items rather than many cheaper quality pieces. The basic essentials include a rubber glove or curry comb for shorthaired Weimaraners, a soft brush and a fine-tooth metal comb for longhaired dogs, a nail-cutting tool, and a toothbrush (see page 76).

TOYS
It is best to purchase some toys especially for your Weimaraner puppy. Your local pet shop will have a good selection, although be wary of some of the toys that are for sale. Weimaraners think squeaky toys are fun, but you will reach screaming point with the incessant noise. Weimaraners are notorious for their determination and can squeak for hours on end. It is wise to buy more than one toy, but only one with a squeak, for the sake of your family's sanity. It is also important to be aware of the temperament of this determined breed. A Weimaraner may wonder where the squeak is coming from and tear the toy

A puppy will need a soft brush. In time, you will need a hound glove to keep the adult coat in good condition.
lynn@kipps.co.uk

apart to find the offending noise. In the process, he could swallow pieces of the toy, which could cause a blockage. The result could be lethal and will certainly involve large vet bills. There are manufacturers that produce sturdy rubber toys, which are virtually indestructible; it can save heartbreak and money in the long run to invest in this sort of product.

Personally, I am not a fan of tugging toys. I believe it encourages peer pressure: the dog learns to tighten his jaws in play, as he grips one end and tussles with his 'mate' on equal terms. His thinking should be that all toys and bones belong to you, but you are kind enough to let him have them.

Small balls should not be used.

If a dog leaps into the air to catch a ball, gravity could drop the ball into the back of the mouth, blocking the air supply.

A toy that is inexpensive and gives hours of fun is an old sock stuffed full of other old socks and knotted securely. It is safe to throw and can be played with safely. It is often remarked that it can be the cheapest toys that give the most pleasure – and a sock is no exception.

CHEWS
Puppies love to chew, but care must be taken when buying things for him to gnaw on. Hide chews are a good choice for Weimaraners, as are compressed minced hide chews, all of which come in various shapes and sizes. These chews, if swallowed whole, represent no hazard to the dog, as they should dissolve in his digestive system without causing any blockages.

Dogs in general love the hoof shavings that the farrier leaves behind after shoeing a horse. These are in small pieces and create no problems. However, full cow hooves are not a good idea, as these could be swallowed and cause a blockage. I prefer to buy Nylabones, which promote healthy teeth and gums. This type of bone can be quite large, but it is useful for a puppy to chew on when teething.

A puppy will enjoy playing with toys – but he can be very destructive.

lynn@kipps.co.uk

ID

Your Weimaraner will need to carry some form of identification. This can be a disc attached to the collar, but you may also wish to consider a permanent form of ID. These days, lots of people opt for microchipping, which provides a permanent and safe way of confirming your pet's identity. If your dog is lost and is taken to a dog warden or a rescue centre, he will be scanned for a microchip, and you will be quickly reunited. Implanting a microchip is a simple procedure, which is carried out by a vet. Another alternative is to tattoo your pet. This takes the form of a permanent marking, usually in the ear.

FINDING A VET

The best way to discover which vet to use is by recommendation.

Obviously this is not always possible, so call into the surgery and talk to the receptionist. Is he or she reassuring, professional, and caring in attitude? Is the waiting room clean with a good atmosphere, or does it give the impression of being a shop only intent in making money? Of course, vets are highly trained and rightly command worthy fees for their expertise but "Are you insured?" should perhaps not be the first thing you are asked.

As a breeder, I encourage new owners to make an appointment with a vet soon after collecting a puppy. A responsible breeder will want to know, as quickly as possible, if something is amiss with a puppy. It also provides an opportunity to seek advice about worming and vaccination programmes. If, at this early stage, you are discontented with

the vet or the service you receive, you have time to look around for another practice where you feel more comfortable. It is essential to establish a good relationship with a vet right from the start.

COLLECTING YOUR PUPPY

The day has finally arrived when you are due to pick up your new puppy from the breeder and bring him home. You may well feel apprehensive, much the same as when you bring a new baby home. In fact, it is a very similar scenario, and your chief concern will probably be: "Will I be able to cope?" The answer is an emphatic 'yes', as long as you have the support of your puppy's breeder, who will be only too happy to help and advise, and to alleviate any insecurities you may have.

It is a good idea to arrange to collect your puppy in the

After all the hard work of rearing a litter, it is time for the breeder to say goodbye to the puppies. *lynn@kipps.co.uk*

morning, as this will give him the rest of the day to settle into his new home. In all the excitement, make sure you have the correct paperwork to go with your puppy. This should include:

- A detailed diet
- Worming programme to date
- Written information on early socialisation
- A pedigree
- Kennel Club papers for transfer of ownership
- Contract of sale.

The contract will vary between breeders, but read it carefully, as it will stipulate the terms of purchase and the support that the breeder is offering, such as taking the puppy back if, in future, circumstances change within the family. You will be advised to take the puppy to

meet the vet at the most convenient opportunity. No caring breeder wants to sell a puppy with health problems, so it is advisable to have the puppy checked early so that if there is anything amiss, it can be detected before you have formed a relationship with your pup. Remember, we are working with nature, not manufacturing a component, and occasionally unforeseen problems may arise.

Taking your puppy to the vet also instigates your initial relationship with the vet, and will, hopefully, confirm that you have confidence in the veterinary practice. You can also discuss a vaccination programme and an ongoing worming programme (see Chapter Eight: Happy and Healthy).

The breeder will also give a supply of food for you to feed

initially. This will avoid too much change when the puppy is settling into his new home. Times of feeding can be changed to fit in with your lifestyle. After all, a puppy has only lived with his mum and littermates for about eight weeks, and is, hopefully, going to spend the next 14 or so years with you.

THE JOURNEY HOME

When you collect your puppy from the breeder, you should take a towel and a roll of kitchen paper. You can also take a blanket, a large cardboard box to travel in, some chews, a collar, newspapers and perhaps a little drink of milk. However, all you really need is a towel in case the puppy dribbles or drools, and kitchen paper in case of accidents on the way home. The rest can wait until he gets home.

ARRIVING HOME

If you were arriving home with a new baby, you would give you and your little one a few days before inviting friends and relatives to inspect the new arrival. Try to give your puppy the same consideration. Remember that his circumstances have changed completely and he needs stability and continuity until he is secure in his new surroundings. If you deal sympathetically with the situation, your relationship with him will be on a sound footing straightaway.

INTRODUCING THE CRATE

It is important to introduce your puppy to his crate so that he knows that this is his 'home base'. Let him settle in his new home and explore (with you overseeing his progress). As he gains confidence that you love him, he will interact with you, starting to play. With all this stress and excitement, he will tire, and this is a good time to pop him in his crate to have a rest. Put something inside the crate to comfort him, perhaps a toy that he has played with or a small blanket that smells of his mum. Stay in the same room, but do not make a fuss of him. This takes the edge off the puppy being shut in his crate and he will soon fall asleep.

The first night that the puppy is put in his crate, it is a good idea to leave a night light on or a radio, so the puppy does not feel deserted. He may well cry for a few nights, because he is used to

Give your puppy plenty of reassurance as he explores his surroundings.
lynn@kipps.co.uk

Once a Weimaraner is accustomed to his crate, he will look on it as his special den.

DIGESTIVE UPSETS

Your puppy will have spent his first eight weeks of life with his mother and siblings, so the change of a new home and family is bound to cause a certain amount of stress – not necessarily bad stress, but the puppy has got to adapt to a whole new world. This probably will result in the puppy having loose motions. Obviously, you will be concerned, but this can make the puppy more anxious. Taking your puppy to the vet could exacerbate the problem, as the vet will be obliged to treat the puppy, even though he is probably not showing any other signs of ill health, such as a raised temperature. In most cases, the puppy will be prescribed an emulsion to ease the diarrhoea, and the vet may suggest a change of diet. All this will irritate the condition further.

If your puppy has loose motions, the first port of call should be the breeder, who will have dealt with this situation on numerous occasions. A few light meals of boiled rice and tuna in brine, or cooked chicken will generally rectify the situation. The breed is not prone to digestive problems – having owned Weimaraners since 1976, I can honestly say that we have never had digestive problems. The crucial point is that we do not worry. We do not dissect what our dogs pass; we merely take note if a motion is not as firm as expected, monitor the dogs and only take action if one appears to show signs of being unwell. For more information on puppy feeding, see Chapter Five: The Best of Care.

sleeping with his littermates. The best plan is to warn the neighbours, have a large drink and leave him to it. Work on the principle that one of you will give in – and it must not be you. Once your puppy settles in his crate, it will give him a sense of security, in the same way that a baby takes comfort from being in a cot. I remember when my children were old enough for a big bed; the lack of security of the bars of the cot made for a testing time.

MEETING THE FAMILY
It is essential to teach a puppy how to behave with children.

Likewise, children should be taught to respect the puppy and not to abuse him by treating him like a plaything. To a child, a puppy is like a living, interacting, cuddly stuffed toy, warm and huggable – and they can learn invaluable lessons if you are on hand to supervise.

From the start, children must learn to respect the fact that the dog is a living animal. It is fun to play with a new puppy or an adult dog, but children must not be rough. Small children have a natural desire to pull a puppy's front legs and tail. Even worse, they pull apart the front legs as if the puppy were a teddy bear.

This is obviously very uncomfortable for the pup, but it is also highly dangerous, as the heart is suspended in the chest, and a fatal injury could result.

When a puppy has settled into his new surroundings, members of the family can sit with him and stroke him kindly – children included – but not for too long. A child should not pick up the puppy, as if the child squeezes too hard, or the puppy becomes bored, he will leap from the arms and could damage himself.

Puppies will play by mouthing each other, rather like children pulling each other in play. With siblings this is fine, with humans not at all, so don't allow children to wind the puppy up into excitement or annoyance so that he reacts by nipping or snapping. If, during play, a puppy does start to grab or snap, tell him "No", using a firm tone of voice. If he persists, hold him until calm, and, when he is relaxed again, tell him how good he is.

Children love puppies and will play constantly. Therefore, it is important to put puppy where he can rest undisturbed. This is where an indoor kennel comes into its own – and children should be taught to leave the pup when he is in his haven.

A dog can be taught black and white rules, but a child is a freethinking human who may forget that respect is important. Mistreatment can turn an amenable, loving pup into one with an aggressive nature, so never take chances and always supervise all child-dog interactions.

MEETING THE RESIDENT DOG

Sometimes people bring the resident family dog with them when they collect their puppy. On the journey home, it is best if an adult sits with the dog and the puppy. This ensures the older dog does not feel left out, and the puppy will get confidence from his presence.

If the first meeting is to take place at your house, take both the pup and the resident dog into the garden so the older dog can show the puppy round his home environment. An older dog can be a little afraid of this small, active

If you supervise early interactions, there is no reason why an adult and a puppy will not become the best of friends. *lynn@kipps.co.uk*

'nuisance' rushing around, often grabbing at his underside, which is how a pup would behave with his mother. So make sure you supervise their initial interactions, and once the dog and puppy have worked out their relationship, they will become firm friends.

Problems are only likely to arise if a pecking order is not established, or if the older dog has an insecure temperament. A well-balanced older dog will quickly realise that a puppy poses no threat. Our dogs spend their days playing together in a fenced paddock. There are often 12 to 15 dogs of all ages and both sexes, but we can put an eight-week-old straight into the paddock with the gang with no ill effects. This is because our dogs are secure in us, bred correctly and reared with love.

If you take your puppy into the garden at regular intervals, he will soon learn what is required.   *lynn@kipps.co.uk*

HOUSE TRAINING

When your puppy first arrives home let him explore the garden. Stay outside with puppy, but ignore him, giving him no distractions. When he performs, you can give him lots of praise and this is the first step in teaching your puppy to toilet outside.

Training is always best done in a positive way with praise. Your puppy will quickly learn that going outside to relieve himself gains positive attention from you. During house training, when puppy performs, always use the same command, such as "Be clean". If you are consistent, the puppy will associate the command with going to the toilet, thus relieving himself on command. When this is achieved, an area can be designated for toileting purposes, so that your garden can be kept clean with minimum effort.

The crate is an excellent training aid. If a puppy never fouls the floor or chews the home, he does not have to be corrected and neither does he form bad habits. We do not advise putting fleece at one end of the crate and paper for fouling at the other end, as this is saying that you condone fouling the bed. A puppy will get the message much quicker if you just put fleece in the crate. When you get up in the morning, open the crate and take your puppy straight out to relieve himself. There will probably a dreadful mess in the crate, but it is not harming your property.

Once outside, hang around quietly – why not take the newspaper out there with you? The aim is for the puppy to lose interest in trying to catch your attention and settle to the job in hand. When he performs, gently praise him. This teaches him that if he toilets in his crate, no one cares and he gets no attention. But if he goes outside, he gets lots of attention and fuss.

Toilet training can be surprisingly quick if you are vigilant, consistent, positive and dismissive of accidents. Often owners are really on the ball with a new puppy, thinking for him: taking him out when he wakes up, when he has eaten, when he stops playing and starts slowly sniffing and then rotating in small circles – all sure signs that he may wish to relieve himself. As a puppy develops the routine of going out to the garden, you can become complacent and expect too much of him. A puppy may be lazy or forgetful, or maybe it is raining, so he squats inside the house. In your frustration, you become agitated, both with him and yourself. This distresses your puppy, as Weimaraners pick up on moods quickly, and the pattern changes and he starts going inside. If this occurs, you will need to start from the beginning again, praising when he performs outside and ignoring him when he has accidents in the home. A Weimaraner responds to praise and positive action; he gains nothing from indifferent response. In fact, this is a good philosophy for all training.

HANDLING A WEIMARANER PUPPY

It is important that your puppy gets used to routine care and handling from an early age.

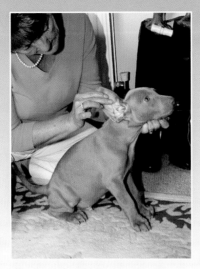

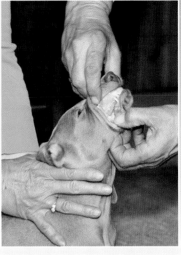

To start with, groom your puppy for a few minutes only.

The ears should be examined to ensure they are clean.

lynn@kipps.co.uk

Check the teeth and the gums – you can reward your puppy with a treat as soon as he co-operates.

HANDLING

A puppy needs regular grooming and must get used to being handled. Each day, you can groom him with a soft brush or rubber glove. To begin with, groom him for no longer than a few minutes so the pup does not become bored and resentful. Eyes can be wiped with cotton wool moistened in boiled cool water. Make sure you use a separate piece of cotton wool for each eye to avoid contamination. The ears can also be wiped using damp cotton wool.

It is a good idea to clean your puppy's teeth from an early age so that he gets used to the procedure. The same applies to trimming nails – but be careful just to take off the tips. If you leave nail trimming until your puppy is older, you will end up having a major struggle. I have heard some vets advise that the nails will wear down naturally if a dog is exercised on hard surfaces, but this is not always the case. The best plan is to start nail trimming while your puppy is young so that he thinks nothing of it. If you do not heed this advice, you will repent at leisure. All these acts of good husbandry will become familiar to the growing dog and make for a stress-free life.

HOUSE RULES

When a new puppy arrives in his new home, you must take on the role of pack leader and protector so that your puppy will look to you for guidance and support. Be reassuring yet confident in showing your puppy what is considered right and wrong in his new home. Obviously, the puppy will spend lots of time in the freedom of the home and, in good weather, the garden. This is why you have him. When he is out playing and learning, you can

If you take on an older dog, you will need to establish a routine so that he learns to settle in his new home.

oversee where his curiosity takes him. In fact, much of his training will be developed by play.

If you want your puppy to be restricted from specific areas of the house, make use of baby or stair gates. This gives you control without confrontation. If puppy is given rules of boundaries while he is tiny, he will not think to change them when he is big enough to jump the baby/stair gate.

When everyone settles down in an evening to watch TV or read, if your puppy wants to be close, why not sit on the floor? If he is never allowed to sit on the sofa, he never will. In our kitchen we have a leather sofa,

which has no buttons or adornments. We do not allow the dogs on to the sofa but recently we felt an older bitch needed extra comfort. We put fleece bedding on the sofa, and told her she was allowed up. At 10 years old, she now knows this is acceptable. However, none of the other dogs ever attempt to climb on to the sofa but they are very happy to curl up on their padded beds. This proves how clever and trainable the breed is. One can change the rules in adulthood – but never in a puppy, or he will take advantage.

It is a puppy's nature to seek attention, and this is something you need to guard against. For

example, if your puppy is playing in the garden, and you rush out to scold him for digging or pulling up plants, he has your instant attention. Therefore, he will probably go out to the garden, looking for mischief, as he knows this gets an instant reaction. The best way to avoid this type of problem is to go out with a toy or a treat and gain his attention. You can reward the puppy for coming to you, and you have distracted him from his 'gardening' activities.

TAKING ON A RESCUED DOG

A rescued dog needs careful guidance in order to settle into a new home. When people bring a rescued dog to be rehomed and you ask the reason, the answer is always valid, logical, and with regret. The truth can often be different. It is human nature not to admit failure or fault. So taking on a rescued dog is a learning process. In many instances, the original owner has not done the groundwork, has failed to understand the breed fully, and has not given clear guidelines to the dog from the start. Then, when the dog becomes a 'teenager', he starts to take control, and the owner realizes that this is not a cute grey bundle with appealing blue eyes, but a strong, self-assured animal who is questioning the pack leader (owner) for dominance.

If you take on a dog that does not know the ground rules, you must be confident, clear and calm in your actions, winning

the mental battle without confrontation. For instance, if your dog climbs on the sofa and you ask him to get down, he may say, to himself: "I have always sat here and I am not about to change now." The most effective way of achieving a positive result is to get a toy he loves or a food treat and show him what you have, but act as if you don't care whether he wants it or not. The dog will think: "Yes, I do want what you are offering." When he comes to get the prize, praise him and perhaps put an obstacle on the sofa so he physically cannot get back on it. So you have won the battle for

supremacy, without confrontation; no one has had to back down or get hurt.

It can be that a rescued dog is so relieved to know where he stands that he relaxes immediately and the confident new owner never sees why he needed to be rehomed.

Rescue organisations work tirelessly to make sure a dog goes to the right environment, so that he is not disrupted mentally. Some people have an idealistic view of giving a poor dog a home; others think it is a cheaper way of getting the breed they want. Many feel that an older dog makes life easier, as house

training etc. has been done. None of these reasons is valid, as a rescued dog can cost more – both mentally and in monetary terms – if he is destructive.

However, if the environment is suitable, you can achieve positive results and enormous pleasure from a dog who has come to you through rescue. You can watch him become confident, bonding with you so that he forgets his negative past. We have seen a dog come to us for rehoming, feeling confused and insecure, and when we have found a caring home we have had the joy of watching the dog develop and blossom with his new owners.

THE BEST OF CARE

5

Chapter

When you are caring for a Weimaraner, you should consider yourself as the first expert, followed by the vet, the food expert and the trainer. Each of these expert roles has different priorities, and it is all too easy to feel baffled, trying to work out what is best for your Weimaraner.

A vet is an expert at dealing with illness and injuries, but he or she is no more a nutritionist than a family doctor. A food merchant will have a variety of products that he or she will want to sell, as profit margins must be maintained. However, you need to be aware that sensitivity within different breeds will dictate proteins levels, so it is not always the most expensive that will work for the Weimaraner. A trainer will have a breed (or breeds) that they work well with, but Weimaraners

are not your average Labrador or compliant Border Collie.

The rule of thumb is to respect your Weimaraner's breeder, who will know the breed intimately and will have experienced all aspects of how the breed thinks and behaves. Obviously, this is on the assumption that you have purchased your puppy from a reputable, experienced breeder. Listen to all the experts, but remember that you are an expert on your individual dog, and you need to find out what works for him.

UNDERSTANDING NUTRITION

While cats are true carnivores, dogs are omnivorous, which means they can feed on vegetable material as well as meat. Feeding dogs in this day and age is so much easier than in previous generations, when you fed meat and crude biscuit or flaked maize.

In those days, dog people relied on instinct in feeding, knowing just the right combination of meat and biscuit by looking at a dog, and knowing the exercise regime to keep the animal in tip-top form.

Today there are still people who swear by the old-fashioned methods. For example, many hunt kennels and big working gundog kennels feed raw, uncleaned tripe. But while this may be acceptable for kennel dogs, the smell of the food and the smell emitted from the dog after feeding can be unacceptable in a dog living in the home as part of the family. There is also the worry of uncooked meat containing various growth additives, which are added to farm animals and/or their feeds to fatten the animal quickly for the table. Likewise, chickens can carry viruses, which could pose a threat to health.

A dog needs a well-balanced diet that is suited to his energy requirements.

David Tomlinson

The big pet food companies taken the guessing out of feeding our animals, and the diets provided are convenient and easy to use. However, it is important to understand what a dog needs to stay fit and healthy in order to ensure you are feeding the right diet for age, lifestyle and breed.

Basically, dogs need the following nutrients:

- **Protein:** for growth, energy and maintenance of body tissue
- **Fat/oil:** for energy and to help the absorption of vitamins A, D, E and K
- **Carbohydrates:** as a filler and fibre provider
- **Vitamins and minerals:** All dogs require certain vitmains and minerals, such as zinc, iron, magnesium, B vitamins, etc. However, a complete diet will already contain these in the right proportions, so it is important not to add them.

It is essential to get the correct balance of these nutrients, and this is where the big well-known dog food companies benefit us. Thousands of pounds are invested in research, and the resulting products are balanced to suit a dog's needs at each stage of development.

As a general rule, a puppy and junior requires between 25-35 per cent protein for growth and development. For the average family pet on a maintenance diet, 18-20 per cent is adequate. People often give their pet too high a protein food, which results in hyperactivity, loose motions, sometimes even aggressive behaviour. If you were to equate a Weimaraner with a horse, you would say a Weimaraner is the thoroughbred of the canine world. If you want a thoroughbred racehorse to win the Derby, you would feed a high-protein diet. If you were to do the same with a Weimaraner, it would have the effect of winding him up to such an extent that you over-exercise him to reduce his over-activity. This forms a vicious circle – the more the dog gets, the more the dog needs.

For a working dog or a pregnant bitch, the protein and fat levels should be higher than a maintenance diet, usually in the region of 28-35 per cent. In an older dog, the levels change again. As activity decreases, the energy required from food decreases. Ideally, a veteran dog requires a lower protein level than a maintenance diet, with slightly reduced fat level and a higher fibre content.

PUPPY FEEDING

If you have chosen an experienced, responsible breeder, they will supply you with a diet sheet, and possibly a sample of the diet, when you collect your puppy. Every breeder will have a preference regarding the diet and the manufacturer, based on their own personal experience. In fact, every breed will thrive on different food product regimes. The Weimaraner is not a chunky, heavy growing puppy, such as a Labrador Retriever. He is more the racehorse, and will therefore grow leggy, rangy and lean. Both mentally and physically he is sensitive to outside influences, much the same as a child who has a high

When first feeding a puppy, follow the breeder's directive.

Keith Allison

metabolic rate, and therefore he can eat great quantities and never appears to put on weight.

When feeding a puppy, follow the breeder's directive in order to have some continuity. Very soon, you can start a routine that will shape your puppy's feeding habits into your lifestyle. Pet food manufacturing is big business, and we are encouraged to start with the puppy food, progressing to a junior food, invariably followed by growth, activity, sensitive, obesity, veteran, gluten-free, and various others advised by the manufacturer. However, when bringing up a baby, we feed our own diet when he or she is ready for solid food, so why would we not feed our puppy in the same way? We could, in effect, go straight to an adult food without detriment to puppy's growth.

Because of the way the breed develops, it is hard to overfeed a growing Weimaraner. I find that feeding as much as the youngster will eat, without over-facing, will not make for an overweight Weimaraner. A point to remember: an eight-week-old puppy's tummy is very small, and a handful of food is probably sufficient for one meal. In order for a puppy to retain his desire to eat, give a small meal, increasing only at the next meal if all food is eaten hungrily. The breeder may have been given a milk drink following solid food, but after eight weeks a puppy's digestion changes so that milk is not a necessary requirement, and may cause loose motions.

Always feed your puppy in the same place, on his own, and without distractions. The Weimaraner is so inquisitive that

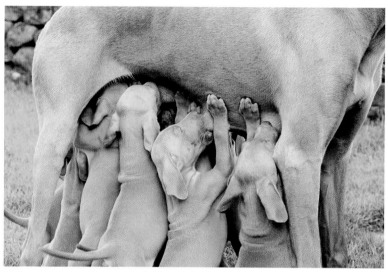

Weimaraner puppies are enthusiastic feeders from birth onwards.

lynn@kipps.co.uk

if you stand and watch him eat, he will nibble at his food and keep looking up at you to see if there is something more interesting going on. A puppy that snacks on his food and then pops over for a cuddle will think he can eat and leave, just as he fancies. But you want to encourage him to retain the eat-or-die principle, which he was born with and which he developed fully whilst vying with his littermates in the pack.

If a puppy is given no distractions, and his food is taken away after an allotted time, he will develop the conditioning to eat at specific times, and in the time allowed. Encouraging a puppy to eat heartily by adding a tempting treat will, in effect, make him fussy. This very intelligent breed will soon realise that if he doesn't eat, his worried owner will add a delicacy.

FEEDING REGIMES

We initially bred English Setters. This breed thinks in a totally different way to the Weimaraner. This was highlighted to us when we bred our first litter of Weimaraner puppies. When English Setter puppies are born, the mum cleans them up and they squeal until the breeder physically hooks them on to the teats. Weimaraner whelps immediately head for the teat and latch on, sucking heartily while mum tries to clean them. Each puppy chooses a teat that he sticks with, so if only three whelps are born, the other teats dry up. If 10 puppies are born, all the teats are used and the puppies learn when to feed.

PROGRESS CHART

- By three weeks of age, the puppies are taking more of an interest in their surroundings and they need a supplement, which usually takes the form of puppy porridge. Initially, there is more porridge on the pups than is eaten, and the dam has a busy job cleaning her babies up.
- By four weeks of age, the puppies understand what a feeding bowl means – and they all dive in together.
- By five weeks, as soon as they hear you coming with food, they are immediately ready to dive in.
- By six weeks, the puppies are fully weaned and are eating four meals a day of a proprietary complete puppy food.
- At seven weeks of age, interest is more in the supplier of the meal than the food itself.
- By eight weeks, the puppy has passed his exam to untie the shoelaces of a prospective new owner rather than have an interest in his littermates or food.
- By 12 weeks, four meals a day tends to become tedious and a puppy will often eat three meals more heartily.
- By six months, two meals are adequate, and this will be the norm throughout a Weimaraner's life.

CHOOSING A DIET

Feeding complete food is far easier than feeding canned feed and biscuit. With canned meat and biscuit you need to feed the right balance of both to fulfil nutritional requirements.

Canned food and biscuit: A clever Weimaraner may pick out the meat and leave the biscuit.

Complete feed: This fulfils all your dog's nutritional requirements.

Weimaraners are very cute and can pick out the meaty bits, leaving the biscuit. Therefore, it is less of a headache feeding a complete food where every nutrient is formed into a dry, hard nut or shape. This not only fulfils all your dog's needs, but is crunchy, which helps to keep teeth clean and strong. There is no smell, nor does the food go off, so there is no waste. Obviously, fresh, clean water must be readily available for the dog at all times, especially when feeding a dry, complete food.

The only problem with this form of feeding is that it is too easy. We want to give our much-loved pet recognition that we care, and putting a bowl of dry food down is not conductive to this end. Another way of feeding a complete diet is by using a flaked complete food. This usually takes the form of coloured biscuits, flakes and dried meat and looks rather like muesli. It can be fed dry, but is usually mixed with warm water, which makes gravy and a pleasing aroma for the dog.

The drawback of this type of diet is that it is possible to separate out the meaty bits from a complete food, so the dog can become picky. This leads to the owner worrying that the dog is not eating enough and therefore adding a tasty supplement to make the dog eat. The Weimaraner, being very astute, realises that by leaving his food, something more appetising will be added. Then we hear the cry: "My Weimaraner won't eat unless I add chicken…" My husband summed up the scenario, saying:

"My children would eat only chocolate if I let them…" It is exactly the same principle.

No dog will starve himself to death. However, a Weimaraner is extremely stubborn and can hold off eating for a long time, feeling sure that you will give in first. This leads to much tension within the household, particularly when this dog is a much-loved member of your family. The tension flows through to the dog, who then worries, which in turn removes the desire to eat. If you worry at mealtimes, so will your dog. We never have bad eaters because there is always another dog standing by who will clean the dish, given the opportunity. All dogs retain the eat-or-die instinct they are born with; learn from this or you will make a rod for your own back. Weimaraners

Do not allow feeding to become an issue with your Weimaraner.

go through various stages of eating, but usually end up devouring anything and everything.

BARF DIET

Barf stands for Bones and Raw Food or Biologically Appropriate Raw Food, depending on which book you read. This seems to be a new system of feeding from an old way of thinking. The advantages of feeding this type of

diet include the following:

- Teeth are healthier and cleaner, without a build-up of plaque.
- Muscles in the jaw, neck and forequarters are enhanced due to the chewing mechanism
- Stools are firmer with fewer odours.
- Dogs who live in the wild, and therefore eat a natural Barf diet, live longer.
- Psychologically, humans need

to nurture, and preparation of this diet fulfils this requirement in us.

On the down side, perhaps dogs live longer in the wild due to hybrid vigour and a more natural environment. Feeding raw bones, chicken wings, liver and heart and raw vegetation may sound romantic, but in reality mass-produced chickens are invariably given growth hormones among other additives, so the meat you are providing is not entirely 'natural'. Pet food manufacturers have strict regimes for producing food and use only best-quality products.

The choice is yours…

MEALTIMES

I would always feed an adult Weimaraner twice a day, even if the dog were overweight, due to the worry of gastric torsion (see Chapter Eight). For the same reason, we are careful about exercising before or after meals. We tend to avoid taking dogs out for an hour before or after a feed. After having exercise, we do not allow our dogs too much water to drink.

If your dog is carrying too much weight, feed two smaller meals. If he always seems hungry, add raw carrot or cabbage, as these add bulk and provide something to chew, thus alleviating hunger pangs. It is rare for a Weimaraner to be overweight, but this must be avoided, as it can lead to serious health problems.

BONE OF CONTENTION

I am always wary of giving bones to the greedy Weimaraner. A dog can get bored and then swallow large chunks, causing blockages and other problems. So 'if in doubt, do not' is a good rule.

We give white, sterilised bones, from pet suppliers, which are good for keeping a dog occupied, while stimulating the jaw and gastric juices. Knucklebones can be OK, but they can upset the dog's tummy if they are too rich. Hide chews are fine, but we avoid the cow hooves, as these can be swallowed. A Weimaraner will gnaw for so long, become bored, and instead of leaving the offending item, will just swallow it. I know a Weimaraner who did exactly this. By the time the vet had detected the foreign body, peritonitis had set in and the dog could not be saved.

GROOMING

The outward appeal of the Weimaraner is the sleek, fine, silver-grey coat, and an obvious plus point is that the coat is easy to care for. This is highlighted when exercising a dog on a wet day in a muddy field, and on returning home a quick sluicing of the legs and belly and a brisk rub with a towel will bring him back to good order.

My father, who was a great horseman, used to say to me that a good groom was worth more than a bucket of corn – and this relates perfectly to the Weimaraner. A rubber curry comb or body brush is fantastic for keeping the coat in good

A bone should only be given under supervision.

order, stimulating the circulation of the hair follicles, and keeping your charge in immaculate condition. Rubber draws the hair out quite miraculously, so don't be tempted to use the synthetic variety, as this will not have the desired effect. A rub down with your hand will create a good sheen to the coat, as the oil in your hand works well. You can also use a chamois leather to good effect.

I am often asked if Weimaraners suffer from the cold due to their lack of undercoat. In fact, I find that cold affects them less than a heavily coated breed where water hangs in the coat, and therefore the animal stays wet for longer. Again, the sleek, fine coat bodes well for the lack of wet dog smell. Weimaraners are fastidiously clean in nature and will lick themselves or their kennel mate to keep clean.

Bathing is not something that needs to be done on a regular basis, as excessive bathing will remove the natural oils, leaving the coat more vulnerable to scurf and indeed cold. Rather like a young lad, a Weimaraner

Grooming with a body brush keeps the coat clean and stimulates circulation.

EARS

As there is no hair growing in the ear, Weimaraners do not have problems with ears – unlike many coated breeds (spaniels, for example). To keep the ears clean, use a proprietary solution, obtained from your vet, but make sure you use it sparingly. Apply a few drops to the ear externally, massage the ear, and then use a piece of cotton wool to wipe away any resulting debris; I would avoid the use of cotton buds, as it is easy to probe too deeply, which could damage the inner ear.

If your dog starts to shake his head or scratch his ear, he may have contracted ear mites. These are virtually undetectable, but cause great discomfort and added problems. Intense head shaking and scratching can cause a haematoma, where the blood vessel bursts in the earflap, causing swelling. Surgery is required or the ear will shrivel as the blood dries away.

Ears are easily nicked in this active breed and will bleed profusely. Potassium permanganate crystals, obtained from the chemist, can be used on damp cotton wool. When held to the wound, they successfully alleviate the bleeding, but care must be taken, as the crystals tend to stain.

NAILS

A characteristic of the breed is that the Weimaraner uses his front legs to gain attention, by clawing your thigh – or even your face, if you are sitting down.

will jump happily into muddy pools on the coldest of days, but be averse to a warm, clean bath. However, a puppy may require a few baths, especially if he uses a crate to sleep overnight, as he can emerge in a bit of a mess before he has learned to go through the night. If a dog is bathed as a youngster, he will grow up objecting less and probably rather liking it.

When bathing your Weimaraner, use a proprietary dog shampoo. I find the varieties containing tea tree or aloe vera are very kind on the skin. Make sure you don't get shampoo in the eyes and don't let water get into the ears. Be careful not to hold the tail inone position for too long when you are cleaning around the anal area, as, for some reason, dogs can suffer 'dead tail' following a bath. This manifests itself by the tail sticking out at the root and dropping. The dog has no control over the tail; it simply hangs. However, it does correct itself within a day or so, and there is no permanent injury.

Rinse your dog thoroughly, removing all trace of shampoo, and then dry him; a chamois leather is perfect at this stage for drying the dog. If the dog is to be bathed in preparation for a show, this is best done a couple of days before to allow the natural oils to return and give sheen to the coat.

To groom and bathe a longhaired Weimaraner is not that different from grooming a shorthaired dog. However, it pays to buy a metal fine-tooth comb, which not only combs the hair but also pulls out dead hair. It can also be beneficial to use thinning scissors to control hair around the entrance to the ears, under the tail and between the toes, as this can keep the dog clean and more comfortable.

EAR CLEANING

A proprietary ear cleaner can be used on a routine basis.

After applying ear cleaner, the ear should be massaged from the outside.

Finally, use cotton wool to clean the ear, making sure you do not probe too deeply.

NAIL CARE

If a Weimaraner is accustomed to having his nails trimmed, he will tolerate the procedure without fuss.

Some people prefer to use a rotary tool with a grinding stone, such as a Dremmel, to keep the nails in trim.

If you don't like the idea of trimming nails, you can file them, although this will need to be done on a regular basis.

Short nails are therefore a must, not only for the dog's comfort, but also for your own. When we have a litter, we always keep nails trimmed in young puppies. If you keep taking the tip off the nail at regular intervals, the puppy comes to accept it quite happily. If this is not kept up, the nail bed will become long and nails will never be able to be kept short.

If you ask a vet to cut nails, the answer may well be that the dog will wear down his nails naturally when walking on hard ground. In my experience, some do and some don't. However, a vet will certainly not relish wrestling with a large Weimaraner just to cut his nails, so it is best to get your puppy used to the procedure while he is a baby. If you incorporate this into your grooming routine from puppyhood, your Weimaraner will think nothing of it.

There are a number of purpose-designed nail-cutting tools available. Personally, I prefer to use a either a small rotary grinder or a clipper with two opposing cutting edges, rather than a guillotone-style clipper, which only has one cutting blade.

If you look closely at a Weimaraner's nails, you can see the quick, so it is easy to avoid nicking it. However, if accidents happen, keep some potassium permanganate crystals (applied with damp cotton wool) or a styptic pencil to stem the blood.

Routine teeth brushing will prevent the build up of tartar and reduce the incidence of gum disease.

TEETH

As a dual-purpose gundog, it is imperative that the Weimaraner has large, white, well-placed teeth. Teeth can be brushed on a regular basis, and the sooner a puppy is accustomed to this, the easier he will be to handle. Start off brushing your puppy's teeth for no more than five seconds and build up. Always use a toothpaste designed for dogs. There are many flavours available to appeal to your dog.

I find that Nylabones are useful for keeping teeth clean and giving the dog the natural chewing exercise. As well as exercising the jaw, it also increases the blood supply to the gums, ensuring healthy teeth. If tartar does build up on the gums, scaling needs to be done under anaesthetic by the vet in order to avoid disease.

EXERCISING YOUR WEIMARANER

How much exercise does a Weimaraner need? How long is a piece of string? For the Weimaraner, mental stimulation is as necessary as physical exercise, as this is a highly intelligent, questioning breed. A puppy, like a human baby, needs lots of rest. In a home pet environment, a puppy will follow you from room to room, and may not get the rest he needs to grow and develop. This is where the indoor kennel/crate comes into its own.

Lots has been spoken and written on the socialisation requirements of a puppy, but there are other important priorities. Looking at an animal in the wild, after ablutions and breakfast, rest would follow for the remaining part of the morning. This is very evident in our field, where our dogs spend the day. A puppy will divide his time between eating, sleeping and playing – he is certainly not on the go all the time. As a puppy grows, his exercise regime will increase.

An adult Weimaraner will take as much or as little exercise as you wish to give him. The more he has, the more he needs, and you can turn him into the Usain Bolt of the canine world. If an adult is not getting the correct amount of exercise, you would soon know, as he will become like a naughty child looking for mischief. Again, this might occur if he is being fed a diet that is too high in protein – much as if you ate fillet steak at ever meal.

A puppy will enjoy intense periods of activity, but these must be punctuated with times when he can rest undisturbed.
lynn@kipps.co.uk

As stated earlier, mental stimulation is as necessary, if not more so, than physical stimulation. If equated with a child, the Weimaraner would be a very bright kid in the class. If that child were with peers of less academic intelligence, he would be a disruptive influence, but, given education to exploit his attributes, he would blossom. So anything that works the brain of the Weimaraner will make him a more acceptable member of your family. Pure obedience is not to his liking, as this requires repetitive application. With his thinking mind, the Weimaraner will establish what aspects of the task are irrelevant and therefore will not appear to be carrying out errands expected. Show training classes, general socialisation classes and agility training are all less structured and therefore more appealing to the Weimaraner.

WHY BREED?

Producing offspring from a dog you dearly love and admire for companionship, showmanship and working ability is a very natural desire. However, reproduction in dogs, as with humans, requires much thought and dedication.

Letting your bitch have one litter 'because it's good for her' is a fallacy. What she has never had, she will never miss. Neither should having puppies be seen as a cure for false pregnancies. In my experience, if a bitch has false pregnancies prior to a litter, she most certainly will have one on subsequent seasons, usually made worse because she has whelped and produced milk. It is certainly not a good enough reason to breed just because your dog has the best temperament and is lovely to look at.

If you don't want to breed from your bitch, it is advisable to have her spayed. You must, however, weigh up the pros and cons, but spaying can be beneficial in terms of health as well as avoiding the problems of on-going seasons. Some vets feel it is easier to spay a bitch while she is still immature, as her uterus will not be fully developed. I prefer to leave spaying until the bitch has had one full season; she may need her first season to mature her body fully. Early spaying may even hinder this process. If it is done after the first season, the

EXERCISING A WEIMARANER

The challenge is to find a balance between the need for physical exertion and mental stimulation.

A Weimaraner at full stretch is a joy to behold.
lynn@kipps.co.uk

A Weimaraner enjoys interacting with his owner, and a game of retrieve provides a means of using mind and body.
lynn@kipps.co.uk

bitch will be young enough to cope with the stresses and strains involved with relative ease. It is far easier for a one-year-old to get over such an operation than a five-year-old, and it reduces the risk of unwanted pregnancies.

Some people think a bitch loses her personality and vitality, and becomes a staid old lady when she has been spayed. This is totally without foundation. Such a thing might happen as the bitch reaches maturity and settles down naturally, but this would be a coincidence and not connected to the operation itself. Often spayed bitches put on weight, but this is generally caused by overfeeding. Spaying can, in some cases, lead to urinary incontinence in the bitch.

There is always an element of risk involved with any operation, although the risk is generally slight with spaying. If you have no intention of breeding with your bitch, it is a wise solution to a life-long problem.

Likewise in a male, castration will pose no health or psychological problem for the dog; it tends to be the owner that suffers from the ethics of it. Dogs lead normal, healthy and happy lives after castration. Boredom and weight gain are not side effects of the operation, but are due to overfeeding, lack of exercise and under stimulation.

It is worth thinking of having your male castrated at about 10-12 months of age, on veterinary advice, as this is before the dog

Rearing a litter is demanding on a bitch, as well as on the breeder, and is not to be undertaken lightly.

lynn@kipps.co.uk

reaches the adolescent stage when dominance can occur.

CARING FOR THE OLDER DOG
It used to be reckoned that if a Weimaraner lived to 11 or 12 years old, he had reached a good age. However, it is not unusual for the breed to live for 14 years – some even make it to 16. This is possibly something to do with improved nutrition and more advanced health care. Now more

breeders screen for genetic disorders, and insurance cover means that owners will consult vets more readily, knowing the bill will be covered.

The Weimaraner does not tend to become a 'creaking gate' as some breeds. This is quite a lean breed that is athletic in conformation, and therefore not prone to becoming overweight. This limits the amount of pressure put on skeletal construction or vital organs.

A Weimaraner's needs will change as he grows older. *lynn@kipps.co.uk*

An older dog may be keen on his food, but he may be slower to eat, so make sure that younger canines in the household don't steal his food. Most of the time, younger dogs show great respect to an older member of their pack, but bear in mind that you are 'pack leader' ultimately, just in case of potential peer pressure.

Hearing and sight may diminish, and, as a result, the old dog can become a little less patient, especially with giddy, young children, You will need to be even more vigilant to ensure the old dog is not startled, which may cause him to snap.

Our older canine friends have a certain charm, which gives so much pleasure. An older bitch of ours started to lose her memory and would demand her tea 10 minutes after she had eaten. If we laughed too loud, she would rush around as if she had been told off, and then she would enjoy even more cuddles than as a youngster. Oh such joy they give!

LETTING GO

The worst thing about owning a dog is that, as with all living things, he will get old and will ultimately die. It says a lot for the dog that you can feel such sorrow and have so many warm memories after sharing such a relatively short time together.

So how do you decide when to let your much-loved pet go with peace? So many times we look at an oldie, thinking, "No she's OK; look, she is wagging her tail", even though her quality of life has gone. We cling to small signs

Desire is prominent in this breed, so if you ask him to accompany you on a long walk, he will forget his age, aches and pains. You will need to think for him; take him out for interesting walks, but cut down on the distance. Make sure his bed is comfortable and well padded so he has a comfortable place to rest.

Most prominent dog food manufacturers produce a range of food that includes a feed specifically for the older dog. Traditionally, protein levels would be reduced; the thinking being that the dog needs less energy as his activity levels decrease. However, recent research has found that protein should be increased, as it maintains lean muscle mass. Within these life-stage foods, supplements to aid mobility and good joint health are often included. The foods are also usually easier to chew and to digest.

In time you will be able to look back and remember all the happy times you spent with your beloved Weimaraner.

lynn@kipps.co.uk

of positives, in otherwise stress-filled negatives – today he enjoyed that tasty morsel, even though he struggled to go out to the garden.... With our canines, we have the ability to relieve suffering because we love them enough. However, it is so hard to see the signs when our thoughts are clouded by love and memories.

To help us find the strength to do the right thing, it is helpful to introduce a third party. This should be someone we trust and respect, who can see the true situation with objectivity. I remember, many years ago, we had an English Setter called Susie. She was the first we'd bred, and she introduced us to the joys of dog showing and winning; she was there when our children were born, and she watched them grow up – there were so many special moments that Susie shared with us. With advanced years and chronic illness, we clung to the flashes of positive moments she still had, not daring to face the inevitable. A good friend called one Sunday morning, and over coffee she gently said that Susie was suffering and the time had come... We called our vet, who came straight away. Susie lay on the rug and went to sleep, released from her pain. We are eternally grateful to our friend; she taught us a life lesson. Susie remains with us in warm memories, as do all our wonderful pets.

In other circumstances, a good and honest vet, with whom you have a long and trusting relationship, can be of great help. He or she will assess the situation, and will know what is best. The pain of losing a much-loved companion is powerful, but the happy memories last a lifetime.

TRAINING AND SOCIALISATION

Chapter 6

When you decided to bring a Weimaraner into your life, you probably had dreams of how it was going to be: long walks together, cosy evenings with a Weimaraner lying devotedly at your feet, and whenever you returned home, there would always be a special welcome waiting for you.

There is no doubt that you can achieve all this – and much more – with a Weimaraner, but, like anything that is worth having, you must be prepared to put in the work. A Weimaraner, regardless of whether he is a puppy or an adult, does not come ready trained, understanding exactly what you want and fitting perfectly into your lifestyle. A Weimaraner has to learn his place in your family and he must discover what is acceptable behaviour.

We have a great starting point in that the Weimaraner has an outstanding temperament. The breed was developed to be an obedient all-round working gundog; he likes to be with people and wants to please them. He is also highly intelligent; he is quick to learn, but you must be on your mettle in order to bring out the best in him.

THE FAMILY PACK

Dogs have been domesticated for some 14,000 years, but, luckily for us, they have inherited and retained behaviour from their distant ancestor – the wolf. A Weimaraner may never have lived in the wild, but he is born with the survival skills and the mentality of a meat-eating predator who hunts in a pack. A wolf living in a pack owes its existence to mutual co-operation and an acceptance of a hierarchy, as this ensures both food and protection. A domesticated dog living in a family pack has exactly the same outlook. He wants food, companionship, and leadership – and it is your job to provide for these needs.

YOUR ROLE

Theories about dog behaviour and methods of training go in and out of fashion, but in reality, nothing has changed from the day when wolves ventured in from the wild to join the family circle. The wolf (and equally the dog) accepts a subservient place in the family pack in return for food and protection. In a dog's eyes, you are his leader, and he relies on you to make all the important decisions. This does not mean that you have to act like a dictator or a bully. You are accepted as a leader, without argument, as long as you have the right credentials.

Do you have what it takes to be a firm, fair and consistent leader?

lynn@kipps.co.uk

The first part of the job is easy. You are the provider, and you are therefore respected because you supply food. In a Weimaraner's eyes, you must be the ultimate hunter because a day never goes by when you cannot find food. The second part of the leader's job description is straightforward, but for some reason we find it hard to achieve. In order for a dog to accept his place in the family pack, he must respect his leader as the decision-maker. A low-ranking pack animal does not question authority; he is perfectly happy to see someone else shoulder the responsibility. Problems will only arise if you cut a poor figure as leader and the dog feels he should mount a challenge for the top-ranking role.

HOW TO BE A GOOD LEADER

There are a number of guidelines to follow to establish yourself in the role of leader in a way that your Weimaraner understands and respects. If you have a puppy, you may think you don't have to take this on board for a few months, but that would be a big mistake. With a Weimaraner it is absolutely essential to start as you mean to go on. The behaviour he learns as a puppy will continue throughout his adult life, which means that undesirable behaviour can be very difficult to rectify. When your Weimaraner first arrives in his new home, follow these guidelines:

• **Keep it simple:** Decide on the rules you want your Weimaraner to obey and always make it 100 per cent clear what is acceptable, and what is unacceptable, behaviour.

• **Be consistent:** If you are not consistent about enforcing rules, how can you expect your Weimaraner to take you seriously? There is nothing worse than allowing your Weimaraner to jump up at you one moment and then scolding him the next time he does it because you were wearing your best clothes. As far as the dog is concerned, he may as well try it on because he can't predict your reaction. Bear in mind, inconsistency leads to insecurity.

You want your dog to give you love and affection, but he must also show respect. *lynn@kipps.co.uk*

- **Get your timing right:** If you are rewarding your Weimaraner, and equally if you are reprimanding him, you must respond within one to two seconds otherwise the dog will not link his behaviour with your reaction (see page 89).
- **Read your dog's body language:** Find out how to read body language and facial expressions (see page 86) so that you understand your Weimaraner's feelings and intentions.
- **Be aware of your own body language:** When you ask your Weimaraner to do something, do not bend over him and talk to him at eye level. Assert your authority by standing over him

and keeping an upright posture. You do not have to be six feet tall to control a Weimaraner, but you do need to convey calmness and confidence. You can also help your dog to learn by using your body language to communicate with him. For example, if you want your dog to come to you, open your arms out and look inviting. If you want your dog to stay, use a hand signal (palm flat, facing the dog) so you are effectively 'blocking' his advance.

- **Tone of voice:** Dogs do not speak English; they learn by associating a word with the required action. However, they are very receptive to tone of

voice, so you can use your voice to praise him or to correct undesirable behaviour. If you are pleased with your Weimaraner, praise him to the skies in a warm, happy voice. If you want to stop him raiding the bin, use a deep, stern voice when you say "No".

- **Give one command only:** If you keep repeating a command, or keep changing it, your Weimaraner will think you are babbling and will probably ignore you. If your Weimaraner does not respond the first time you ask, make it simple by using a treat to lure him into position, and then you can reward him for a correct response.

READING CANINE BODY LANGUAGE

A male and a female meeting: The male (right) is standing tall, but giving off friendly signals. The female has adopted a more submissive posture.

Both male and female are more relaxed and they realise that neither is offering a threat.

The male (right) goes into the play position, inviting the female to have a game.

- **Daily reminders:** A young, exuberant Weimaraner is apt to forget his manners from time to time, and an adolescent dog may attempt to challenge your authority (see page 100). Rather than coming down on your Weimaraner like a ton of bricks when he does something wrong, try to prevent bad manners by daily reminders of good manners. For example:
  i   Do not let your dog barge ahead of you when you are going through a door.
  ii Do not let him leap out of the car the moment you open the door (which could be potentially lethal, as well as being disrespectful).
  iii Do not let him eat from your hand when you are at the table.
  iv Do not let him 'win' a toy at the end of a play session and then make off with it. You 'own' his toys, and you 'allow' him to play with them. Your Weimaraner must learn to give up a toy when you ask.

In all your dealings with a Weimaraner, keeps things simple, calm and positive.

UNDERSTANDING YOUR WEIMARANER

Body language is an important means of communication between dogs, which they use to make friends, to assert status, and to avoid conflict. It is important to get on your dog's wavelength by understanding his body language and reading his facial expressions.

- A positive body posture and a wagging tail indicate a happy, confident dog.
- A crouched body posture with ears back and tail down show that a dog is being submissive. A dog may do this when he is being told off or if a more assertive dog approaches him.
- A bold dog will stand tall, looking strong and alert. His ears will be forward and his tail will be held high.
- A dog who raises his hackles (lifting the fur along his topline) is trying to look as scary as possible. A Weimaraner may do this if he senses a threat, and if he is with his owner, it may well bring out his protective instinct.
- A playful dog will go down on his front legs while standing on his hind legs in a bow position. This friendly invitation says: "I'm no threat, let's play."
- A Weimaraner speciality is striking out with the front legs as a form of greeting, like a human child would run forward with arms outstretched to play fight with a sibling. This is first seen when puppies are interacting with each other in a litter, and it is often seen as a form of attention-seeking behaviour in adult dogs.
- A dominant, aggressive dog will meet other dogs with a hard stare. In the case of a Weimaraner, the eyes will darken perceptibly. This characteristic may also be seen when the dog is excited or fearful. If he is challenged, he may bare his teeth and growl, and the corners of his mouth will be drawn forward. His ears will be forward and he will appear tense in every muscle.
- A nervous dog will often show aggressive behaviour as a means of self-protection. If threatened, this dog will lower his head and flatten his ears. The corners of his mouth may be drawn back, and he may bark or whine.
- Some Weimaraners are 'smilers', curling up their top lip and showing their teeth when they greet people. This should never be confused with a snarl, which would be accompanied by the upright posture of a dominant dog. A smiling dog will have a low body posture and a wagging tail; he is being submissive and it is a greeting that is often used when low-ranking animals greet high-ranking animals in a pack.

GIVING REWARDS

Why should your Weimaraner do as you ask? If you follow the guidelines given above, your Weimaraner should respect your authority, but what about the time when he is playing with a new doggy friend or has found a really enticing scent? The answer is that you must always be the most interesting, the most attractive, and the most irresistible person in your Weimaraner's eyes. It would be

You need to find out what your Weimaraner most values as a reward – in this case it is a toy.

nice to think that you could achieve this by personality alone, but most of us need a little extra help. You need to find out what is the biggest reward for your dog. It may be a food treat, or some Weimaraners prefer a game with a favourite toy, but, whatever it is, it must be something that your dog really wants.

When you are teaching a dog a new exercise, you should reward your Weimaraner frequently. When he knows the exercise or command, reward him randomly so that he keeps on responding to you in a positive manner. If your dog does something extra

special, like leaving his canine chum mid-play in the park, make sure he really knows how pleased you are by giving him a handful of treats or throwing his ball a few extra times. If he gets a bonanza reward, he is more likely to come back on future occasions because you have proved to be even more rewarding than his previous activity.

TOP TREATS
Some trainers grade treats depending on what they are asking the dog to do. A dog may get a low-grade treat, such as a piece of dry food, to reward good behaviour on a random basis,

such as sitting when you open a door or allowing you to examine his teeth. But high-grade treats, which may be cooked liver, sausage or cheese, are reserved for training new exercises or for use in the park when you want a really good recall. Whatever type of treat you use, remember to subtract it from your Weimaraner's daily ration. Weimaraners are not generally prone to obesity, but it is important to bear in mind that fat dogs are lethargic, prone to health problems, and will almost certainly have a shorter life expectancy. Reward your Weimaraner, but always keep a check on his figure!

HOW DO DOGS LEARN?
It is not difficult to get inside your Weimaraner's head and understand how he learns, as it is not dissimilar to the way we learn. Dogs learn by conditioning: they find out that specific behaviours produce specific consequences. This is known as operant conditioning or consequence learning. Consequences have to be immediate or clearly linked to the behaviour, as a dog sees the world in terms of action and result. Dogs will quickly learn if an action has a bad consequence or a good consequence.

Dogs also learn by association. This is known as classical conditioning or association learning. It is the type of learning made famous by Pavlov's experiment with dogs. Pavlov presented dogs with food and

THE CLICKER REVOLUTION

Karen Pryor pioneered the technique of clicker training when she was working with dolphins. It is very much a continuation of Pavlov's work and makes full use of association learning. Karen wanted to mark 'correct' behaviour at the precise moment it happened. She found it was impossible to toss a fish to a dolphin when it was in mid-air, when she wanted to reward it. Her aim was to establish a conditioned response so the dolphin knew that it had performed correctly and a reward would follow.

The solution was the clicker: a small matchbox-shaped training aid, with a metal tongue that makes a click when it is pressed. To begin with, the dolphin had to learn that a click meant that food was coming. The dolphin then

learnt that it must 'earn' a click in order to get a reward. Clicker training has been used with many different animals, most particularly with dogs, and it has proved hugely successful. It is a great aid for pet owners and is also widely used by professional trainers who are teaching highly specialised skills.

measured their salivary response (how much they drooled). Then he rang a bell just before presenting the food. At first, the dogs did not salivate until the food was presented. But after a while they learnt that the sound of the bell meant that food was coming, and so they salivated when they heard the bell. A dog needs to learn the association in order for it to have any meaning. For example, a dog that has never seen a lead before will be completely indifferent to it. A dog that has learnt that a lead means he is going for a walk will get excited the second he sees the lead; he has learnt to associate a lead with a walk.

BE POSITIVE

The most effective method of training dogs is to use their ability to learn by consequence and to teach that the behaviour you want produces a good consequence. For example, if you ask your Weimaraner to "Sit", and reward him with a treat, he will learn that it is worth his while to sit on command because it will lead to a treat. He is far more likely to repeat the behaviour, and the behaviour will become stronger, because it results in a positive outcome. This method of training is known as positive reinforcement, and it generally leads to a happy, co-operative dog that is willing to

work, and a handler who has fun training their dog.

The opposite approach is negative reinforcement. This is far less effective and often results in a poor relationship between dog and owner. In this method of training, you ask your Weimaraner to "Sit", and, if he does not respond, you deliver a sharp yank on the training collar or push his rear to the ground. The dog learns that not responding to your command has a bad consequence, and he may be less likely to ignore you in the future. However, it may well have a bad consequence for you, too. A dog that is treated in this way may associate harsh handling

Find a training area that is free from distractions so that your Weimaraner will focus on you.

with the handler and become aggressive or fearful. Instead of establishing a pattern of willing co-operation, you are establishing a relationship built on coercion.

GETTING STARTED

As you train your Weimaraner, you will develop your own techniques as you get to know what motivates him. You may decide to get involved with clicker training or you may prefer to go for a simple command-and-reward formula. It does not matter what form of training you use, as long as it is based on positive, reward-based methods.

There are a few important guidelines to bear in mind when you are training your Weimaraner:

- Find a training area that is free from distractions, particularly when you are just starting out.
- Keep training sessions short, especially with young puppies that have very short attention spans.
- Do not train if you are in a bad mood or if you are on a tight schedule – the training session will be doomed to failure.
- If you are using a toy as a reward, make sure it is only available when you are training. In this way it has an added value for your Weimaraner.

- If you are using food treats, make sure they are bite-size and easy to swallow; you don't want to hang about while your Weimaraner chews on his treat.
- Do not attempt to train your Weimaraner after he has eaten, or soon after returning from exercise. He will either be too full up to care about food treats or too tired to concentrate.
- When you are training, move around your allocated area so that your dog does not think that an exercise can only be performed in one place.
- If your Weimaraner is finding an exercise difficult, try not to get frustrated. Go back a step and praise him for his effort. You will probably find he is more successful when you try again at the next training session.
- If a training session is not going well – either because you are in the wrong frame of mind or the dog is not focusing – ask your Weimaraner to do something you know he can do (such as a trick he enjoys performing), and then you can reward him with a food treat or a play with his favourite toy, ending the session on a happy, positive note.
- Do not train for too long. You need to end a training session on a high, with your Weimaraner wanting more, rather than making him sour by asking too much from him.

In the exercises that follow, clicker training is introduced and followed, but all the exercises will work without the use of a clicker.

INTRODUCING A CLICKER

This is dead easy, and the intelligent Weimaraner will learn about the clicker in record time! It can be combined with attention training, which is a very useful tool and can be used on many different occasions.

- Prepare some treats and go to an area that is free from distractions. When your Weimaraner stops sniffing around and looks at you, click and reward by throwing him a treat. This means he will not crowd you, but will go looking for the treat. Repeat a couple of times. If your Weimaraner is very easily distracted, you may need to start this exercise with the dog on a lead.
- After a few clicks, your Weimaraner will understand that if he hears a click, he will get a treat. He must now learn that he must 'earn' a click. This time, when your Weimaraner looks at you, wait a little longer before clicking, and then reward him. If your Weimaraner is on a lead but responding well, try him off the lead.
- When your Weimaraner is working for a click and giving you his attention, you can introduce a cue or command word, such as "Watch". Repeat a few times, using the cue. You now have a Weimaraner that understands the clicker and will give you his attention when you ask him to "Watch".

TRAINING EXERCISES

THE SIT

This is the easiest exercise to teach, so it is rewarding for both you and your Weimaraner.

- Choose a tasty treat and hold it just above your puppy's nose. As he looks up at the treat, he will naturally go into the Sit.

As soon as he is in position, reward him.
- Repeat the exercise, and when your pup understands what you want, introduce the "Sit" command.
- You can practise at mealtimes by holding out the bowl and waiting for your dog to sit. Most Weimaraners learn this one very quickly!

Use a treat to lure your Weimaraner into the Sit. In time, he will respond to a voice command and you can reward him on a random basis.

Lower a treat towards the ground and your Weimaraner will follow it, going into the Down position.

Work on getting an enthusiastic response to the Recall.

THE DOWN

Work hard at this exercise because a reliable Down is useful in many different situations, and an instant Down can be a lifesaver.

- You can start with your dog in a Sit, or it is just as effective to teach it when the dog is standing. Hold a treat just below your puppy's nose, and slowly lower it towards the ground. The treat acts as a lure, and your puppy will follow it, first going down on his forequarters, and then bringing his hindquarters down as he tries to get the treat.

- Make sure you close your fist around the treat, and only reward your puppy with the treat when he is in the correct position. If your puppy is reluctant to go Down, you can apply gentle pressure on his shoulders to encourage him to go into the correct position.
- When your puppy is following the treat and going into position, introduce a verbal command.
- Build up this exercise over a period of time, each time waiting a little longer before giving the reward, so the puppy learns to stay in the Down position.

THE RECALL

It is never too soon to begin training the Recall. Ideally the breeder will have already started this by calling the puppies in from outside and rewarding them with some treats scattered on the floor. But even if this has not been the case, you will find that a puppy arriving in his new home is highly responsive. In a puppy's eyes, you are God, and his chief desire is to follow you and be with you. Capitalise on this from day one by getting your pup's attention and calling him to you in a bright, excited tone of voice.

- Practise in the garden. When

SECRET WEAPON

You can build up a strong Recall by using another form of association learning. Buy a whistle, and when you are giving your Weimaraner his food, peep on the whistle. You can choose the type of signal you want to give: two short peeps or one long whistle, for example. Within a matter of days, your dog will learn that the sound of the whistle means that food is coming.

Now transfer the lesson outside. Arm yourself with some tasty treats and the whistle. Allow your Weimaraner to run free in the garden, and, after a couple of minutes, use the whistle. The dog has already learnt to associate the whistle with food, so he will come towards you.

Immediately reward him with a treat and lots of praise. Repeat the lesson a few times in the garden so you are confident that your dog is responding before trying it in the park. Make sure you always have some treats in your pocket when you go for a walk, and your dog will quickly learn how rewarding it is to come to you.

your puppy is busy exploring, get his attention by calling his name, and, as he runs towards you, introduce the verbal command "Come". Make sure you sound happy and exciting, so your puppy wants to come to you. When he responds, give him lots of praise.

- If your puppy is slow to respond, try running away a few paces, or jumping up and down. It doesn't matter how silly you look, the key issue is to get your puppy's attention, and then make yourself irresistible!
- In a dog's mind, coming when called should be regarded as the best fun because he knows he is always going to be rewarded. Never make the

mistake of telling your dog off, no matter how slow he is to respond, as you will undo all your previous hard work.
- When you call your Weimaraner to you, make sure he comes up close enough to be touched. He must understand that "Come" means that he should come right up to you, otherwise he will think that he can approach and then veer off when it suits him.
- When you are free running your dog, make sure you have his favourite toy or a pocket full of treats so you can reward him at intervals throughout the walk when you call him to you. Do not allow your dog to free run and only call him back

at the end of the walk to clip on his lead. An intelligent Weimaraner will soon realise that the Recall means the end of his walk, and then end of fun – so who can blame him for not wanting to come back?

TRAINING LINE
This is the equivalent of a very long lead, which you can buy at a pet store, or you can make your own with a length of rope. The training line is attached to your Weimaraner's collar and should be around 15 feet (4.5 metres) in length.

The purpose of the training line is to prevent your Weimaraner from disobeying you so that he never has the chance to get into bad habits. For example, when

The aim is for your Weimaraner to walk on a loose lead, focusing attention on you when required.

you call your Weimaraner and he ignores you, you can immediately pick up the end of the training line and call him again. By picking up the line you will have attracted his attention, and if you call in an excited, happy voice, your Weimaraner will come to you. The moment he reaches you, give him a tasty treat so he is instantly rewarded for making the 'right' decision.

The training line is very useful when your Weimaraner becomes an adolescent and is testing your leadership. When you have reinforced the correct behaviour a number of times, your dog will build up a strong recall and you will not need to use a training line.

WALKING ON A LOOSE LEAD

This is a simple exercise, which baffles many Weimaraner owners. In most cases, owners are too impatient, wanting to get on with the expedition rather that training the dog how to walk on a lead. Take time with this one; the Weimaraner is a strong dog, and a Weimaraner that pulls on the lead is no pleasure to own.

In this exercise, as with all lessons that you teach your Weimaraner, you must adopt a calm, determined, no-nonsense attitude so your Weimaraner knows that you mean business. This is a dog with considerable mental strength, and you need to earn his respect. Once this is

established, your Weimaraner will take you seriously and be happy to co-operate with you.

- In the early stages of lead training, allow your puppy to pick his route and follow him. He will get used to the feeling of being 'attached' to you, and has no reason to put up any resistance.
- Next, find a toy or a tasty treat and show it to your puppy. Let him follow the treat/toy for a few paces, and then reward him.
- Build up the amount of time your pup will walk with you, and when he is walking nicely by your side, introduce the

verbal command "Heel" or "Close". Give lots of praise when your pup is in the correct position.

- When your pup is walking alongside you, keep focusing his attention on you by using his name, and then rewarding him when he looks at you. If it is going well, introduce some changes of direction.

- Do not attempt to take your puppy out on the lead until you have mastered the basics at home. You need to be confident that your puppy accepts the lead, and will focus his attention on you, when requested, before you face the challenge of a busy environment.

- As your Weimaraner gets bigger and stronger, he may try to pull on the lead, particularly if you are heading somewhere he wants to go, such as the park. If this happens, stop, call your dog to you, and do not set off again until he is in the correct position. It may take time, but your Weimaraner will eventually realise that it is more productive to walk by your side than to pull ahead.

Build up the Stay exercise in easy stages.

STAYS

This may not be the most exciting exercise, but it is one of the most useful. There are many occasions when you want your Weimaraner to stay in position, even if it is only for a few seconds. The classic example is when you want your Weimaraner to stay in the back of the car until you have clipped on his lead. Some trainers use the verbal command "Stay" when the dog is to stay in position for an extended period of time, and "Wait" if the dog is to stay in position for a few seconds until you give the next command. Others trainers use a universal "Stay" to cover all situations. It all comes down to personal preference, and as long as you are consistent, your dog will understand the command he is given.

- Put your puppy in a Sit or a Down, and use a hand signal (flat palm, facing the dog) to show he is to stay in position.

Step a pace away from the dog. Wait a second, step back and reward him. If you have a lively pup, you may find it easier to train this exercise on the lead.

- Repeat the exercise, gradually increasing the distance you can leave your dog. When you return to your dog's side, praise him quietly and release him with a command, such as "OK".

- Remember to keep your body language very still when you are training this exercise, and avoid eye contact with your dog. Work on this exercise over a period of time, and you will build up a really reliable Stay.

WE CAN KEEP GOING ALL DAY

Repetition is often a key element in training a Weimaraner, as he wants to find out who is mentally stronger. For example, you may have a dog who continually tries to jump out of the car when you raise the tailgate. Ideally, you should have stopped this behaviour the moment it started, but if you have neglected to do this, there is still hope.

When your Weimaraner tries to jump out, lower the tailgate, and tell him "No" in a stern voice. He will think the door is closing on him, so he will stay put. Try again, and when your Weimaraner tries to leap out, lower the tailgate, and repeat the reprimand. You may have to do this half a dozen times before your Weimaraner accepts that he must stay in the car, but eventually he will realise that there is no gain in trying to leap out. Do not shout at him or become stressed. The exercise will only work if you remain calm and keep repeating the scenario as if you hadn't a care in the world. Once your Weimaraner realises that you will not give up – even if it takes all day – he will respect you and will do as he is asked.

SOCIALISATION

While your Weimaraner is mastering basic obedience exercises, there is other, equally important, work to do with him. A Weimaraner is not only becoming a part of your home and family, he is becoming a member of the community. He needs to be able to live in the outside world, coping calmly with every new situation that comes his way. It is your job to introduce him to as many different experiences as possible, and to encourage him to behave in an appropriate manner.

In order to socialise your Weimaraner effectively, it is helpful to understand how his brain is developing, and this will help to provide you with a perspective on how he sees the world.

CANINE SOCIALISATION
(Birth to 7 weeks)
This is the time when a dog learns how to be a dog. By interacting with his mother and his littermates, a young pup learns about leadership and submission. He learns to read body posture so that he understands the intentions of his mother and his siblings. A puppy that is taken away from his litter too early may always have behavioural problems with other dogs, either being fearful or aggressive.

SOCIALISATION PERIOD
(7 to 12 weeks)
This is the time to get cracking and introduce your Weimaraner puppy to as many different experiences as possible. This includes meeting different people, other dogs and animals, seeing new sights, and hearing a range of sounds, from the vacuum cleaner to the roar of traffic. At this stage, a puppy learns very quickly and what he learns will stay with him for the rest of his life. This is the best time for a puppy to move to a new home, as he is adaptable and ready to form deep bonds.

FEAR-IMPRINT PERIOD
(8 to 11 weeks)
This occurs during the socialisation period, and it can be the cause of problems if it is not handled carefully. If a pup is exposed to a frightening or painful experience, it will lead to lasting impressions. Obviously, you will attempt to avoid frightening situations, such as your pup being bullied by a

mean-spirited older dog, or a firework going off, but you cannot always protect your puppy from the unexpected. If your pup has a nasty experience, the best plan is to make light of it and distract him by offering him a treat or a game. The pup will take the lead from you and will be reassured that there is nothing to worry about. If you mollycoddle him and sympathise with him, he is far more likely to retain the memory of his fear.

SENIORITY PERIOD
(12 to 16 weeks)
During this period, your Weimaraner puppy starts to cut the apron strings and becomes more independent. He will test out his status to find out who is the pack leader: him or you. Bad habits, such as play biting, which may have been seen as endearing a few weeks earlier, should be firmly discouraged. Remember to use positive, reward-based training, but make sure your puppy knows that you are the leader and must be respected.

SECOND FEAR-IMPRINT
PERIOD (6 to 14 months)
This period is not as critical as the first fear-imprint period, but it should still be handled carefully. During this time your Weimaraner may appear apprehensive, or he may show fear of something familiar. You may feel as if you have taken a backwards step, but if you adopt a calm, positive manner, your Weimaraner will see that there is nothing to be frightened of. Do

One of the first experiences of socialisation is when puppies interact with each other.

not make your dog confront the thing that frightens him. Simply distract his attention, and give him something else to think about, such as obeying a simple command, such as "Sit" or "Down". This will give you the opportunity to praise and reward your dog, and will help to boost his confidence.

YOUNG ADULTHOOD AND MATURITY (1 to 4 years)
The timing of this phase depends on the size of the dog: the bigger the dog, the later it is. This period coincides with a dog's increased size and strength, mental as well as physical. Some dogs, particularly those with a dominant nature, will test your leadership again and may become

aggressive towards other dogs. Firmness and continued training are essential at this time so that your Weimaraner accepts his status in the family pack.

IDEAS FOR SOCIALISATION
When you are socialising your Weimaraner, you want him to experience as many different situations as possible. Try out some of the following ideas, which will ensure your Weimaraner has an all-round education.

If you are taking on a rescued dog and have little knowledge of his background, it is important to work through a programme of socialisation. A young puppy soaks up new experiences like a sponge, but an older dog can still

A well-socialised dog will react calmly and confidently in a variety of different situations.

learn. If a rescued dog shows fear or apprehension, treat him in exactly the same way as you would treat a youngster who is going through the second fear-imprint period (see page 97).

- Accustom your puppy to household noises, such as the vacuum cleaner, the television and the washing machine.
- Ask visitors to come to the door, wearing different types of clothing – for example, wearing a hat, a long raincoat, or carrying a stick or an umbrella.
- If you do not have children at home, make sure your Weimaraner has a chance to

meet and play with them. Go to a local park and watch children in the play area. You will not be able to take your Weimaraner inside the play area, but he will see children playing and will get used to their shouts of excitement.
- Attend puppy classes. These are designed for puppies between the ages of 12 to 20 weeks, and give puppies a chance to play and interact together in a controlled, supervised environment. Your vet will have details of a local class.
- Take a walk around some quiet streets, such as a residential area, so your Weimaraner can

get used to the sound of traffic. As he becomes more confident, progress to busier areas. Remember: your lead is like a live wire, and your feelings will travel directly to your Weimaraner. Assume a calm, confident manner, and your puppy will take the lead from you and have no reason to be fearful.
- Go to a railway station. You don't have to get on a train if you don't need to, but your Weimaraner will have the chance to experience trains, people wheeling luggage, loudspeaker announcements, and going up and down stairs and over railway bridges.

A training class provides a learning environment where your dog must focus on you despite the distraction of other dogs.

- If you live in the town, plan a trip to the country. You can enjoy a day out and provide an opportunity for your Weimaraner to see livestock, such as sheep, cattle and horses.
- One of the best places for socialising a dog is at a country fair. There will be crowds of people, livestock in pens, tractors, bouncy castles, fairground rides and food stalls.
- When your dog is over 20 weeks of age, locate a training class for adult dogs. You may find that your local training class has both puppy and adult classes.

TRAINING CLUBS

There are lots of training clubs to choose from. Your vet will probably have details of clubs in your area, or you can ask friends who have dogs if they attend a club. Alternatively, use the internet to find out more information. But how do you know if any particular club is any good?

Before you take your dog, ask if you can go to a class as an observer and find out the following:

- What experience does the instructor(s) have?
- Do they have experience with Weimaraners?
- Is the class well organised,

and are the dogs reasonably quiet? (A noisy class indicates an unruly atmosphere, which will not be conducive to learning.)
- Are there a number of classes to suit dogs of different ages and abilities?
- Are positive, reward-based training methods used?
- Does the club train for the Good Citizen Scheme (see page 107)?

If you are not happy with the training club, find another one. An inexperienced instructor who cannot handle a number of dogs in a confined environment can do more harm than good.

THE ADOLESCENT WEIMARANER

It happens to every dog – and every owner. One minute you have an obedient well-behaved youngster, and the next you have a boisterous adolescent who appears to have forgotten everything he ever learnt. Both males and females show adolescent behaviour, but it is generally more of an issue with a male Weimaraner.

A Weimaraner male will show adolescent behaviour at any time between eight months and 18 months – in some cases, this may continue until a dog is two years old. Generally, a male will become more assertive as he challenges his position in the pecking order. He will appear bouncy and confident, and will seek any chink in your armour to progress his claim to be top dog.

Female Weimaraners show adolescent behaviour as they approach their first season, which is at around 12 months of age. Just like a female suffering from PMT, a Weimaraner becomes hormonal and her behaviour will change a few weeks before she comes into season. She will rarely attempt to be dominant, but she may be manipulative, only seeking to co-operate when she can see a positive, personal gain. At this time she may be intolerant with other dogs, resenting the attentions of males, and showing a short fuse with other females. Firmness and patience are the best response when dealing with an adolescent female, and she will become easier to live with as soon as her hormone levels have settled.

There are more problems associated with dealing with an adolescent male Weimaraner, and it is a fact that most Weimaraners who end up in rescue are males aged around two years. In most cases, the dog has tried to get the upper hand; the owner has let it happen and is left with a dog that is ruling the roost.

This nightmare scenario can be avoided if you look at the situation from the dog's perspective and give the correct response. Just like a teenager, an adolescent male Weimaraner feels the need to flex his muscles and challenge the status quo. He may become disobedient and break house rules as he tests your authority and your role as leader. Your response must be firm, fair and consistent. If you show that you are a strong leader (see page 84) and are quick to reward good behaviour, your Weimaraner will accept you as his protector and provider.

WHEN THINGS GO WRONG

Positive, reward-based training has proved to be the most effective method of teaching

When a Weimaraner hits adolescence, he may try to test his boundaries.

dogs, but what happens when your Weimaraner does something wrong and you need to show him that his behaviour is unacceptable? The old-fashioned school of dog training used to rely on the powers of punishment and negative reinforcement. A dog who raided the bin, for example, was smacked. Now we have learnt that it is not only unpleasant and cruel to hit a dog, it is also ineffective. If you hit a dog for stealing, he is more than likely to see you as the bad consequence of stealing, so he may raid the bin again, but probably not when you are around. If he raided the bin some time before you discovered it, he will be even more confused by your punishment, as he will not relate your response to his 'crime'.

A more commonplace example is when a dog fails to respond to a recall in the park. When the dog eventually comes back, the owner puts the dog on the lead and goes straight home to punish him for his poor response. Unfortunately, the dog will have a different interpretation. He does not think: "I won't ignore a recall command because the bad consequence is the end of my play in the park." He thinks: "Coming to my owner resulted in the end of playtime – therefore coming to my owner has a bad consequence, so I won't do that again."

There are a number of strategies to tackle undesirable behaviour – and they have nothing to do with harsh handling.

For a Weimaraner, a worst-case scenario is to be ignored.

Ignoring bad behaviour: The Weimaraner is a big, strong, energetic dog, and a lot of undesirable behaviour in youngsters is to do with over-exuberance and lack of respect. For example, a young Weimaraner that mugs visitors when they come to the door is simply fulfilling his desire for attention. Even if he is told off for his over-enthusiastic greeting, he is still getting attention, so why inhibit his behaviour?

In this situation, the best and most effective response is to ignore your Weimaraner. Ideally, you should start this 'training' when your puppy first comes home. If a puppy is allowed to jump up and greet visitors every time they come to the door, he will continue that behaviour into adulthood when it becomes increasingly unpopular. However, if you ask visitors to ignore the puppy when they arrive – no matter how cute he is being – he will not get into the 'mugging' mind set. He will learn that he is greeted when he is being calm, and will see no need to throw himself at everyone that comes through the door.

If your Weimaraner has got into bad habits and has started mugging visitors, you will need to recruit a 'doggy' friend to act as a stooge. When the friend comes to the door, they must be under strict instructions to ignore your Weimaraner – not looking at him, telling him off, or pushing him down. These actions may appear to be negative, but as far as your attention-seeking Weimaraner is concerned, they are all rewarding. But someone who turns their back on him and offers no response is plain boring. The moment your Weimaraner has four feet on the ground, allow your friend to speak to him, and maybe give him a treat. If you repeat this often enough, the Weimaraner will learn that jumping up does not have any good consequences, such as getting attention. Instead he is ignored. However, when he has all four feet on the ground, he gets loads of attention. He links the action with the consequence, and chooses the action that is most rewarding. You will find that this strategy works well with all attention-seeking behaviour, such as barking, whining or scrabbling at doors. Being ignored is a worst-case scenario for a

Despite your best efforts, you may face the challenge of coping with problem behaviour. *lynn@kipps.co.uk*

Weimaraner, so remember to use it as an effective training tool.

Stopping bad behaviour: There are occasions when you want to call an instant halt to whatever it is your Weimaraner is doing. He may have just jumped on the sofa, or you may have caught him red-handed in the rubbish bin. He has already committed the 'crime', so your aim is to stop him and to redirect his attention.

You can do this by using a deep, firm tone of voice to say "No", which will startle him, and then call him to you in a bright, happy voice. If necessary, you can attract him with a toy or a treat. The moment your Weimaraner stops the undesirable behaviour and comes towards you, you can reward his good behaviour. You can back this up by running through a couple of simple exercises, such as a Sit or a Down, and rewarding with treats. In this way, your Weimaraner focuses his attention on you, and sees you as the greatest source of reward and pleasure.

In a more extreme situation, when you want to interrupt undesirable behaviour, and you know that a simple "No" will not do the trick, you can try something a little more dramatic. If you get a can and fill it with pebbles, it will make a really loud noise when you shake it or throw it. The same effect can be achieved with purpose-made training discs. The dog will be startled and stop what he is doing. Even better, the dog will not associate the unpleasant noise with you. This gives you the perfect opportunity to be the nice guy, calling the dog to you and giving him lots of praise.

PROBLEM BEHAVIOUR

If you have trained your Weimaraner from puppyhood, survived his adolescence and established yourself as a fair and consistent leader, you will end up with a brilliant companion dog. The Weimaraner is a well-balanced dog, who is eager to please and rarely has hang-ups. Most Weimaraners are out-going, fun-loving and thrive on spending time with their owners.

However, problems may arise unexpectedly, or you may have taken on a rescued Weimaraner that has established behavioural problems. If you are worried about your Weimaraner and feel out of your depth, do not delay in seeking professional help. This is readily available, usually through a referral from your vet, or you can find out additional information on the internet (see Appendices for web addresses). An animal behaviourist will have experience in tackling problem behaviour and will be able to help both you and your dog.

It is also important to look at your Weimaraner's diet if you are experiencing behavioural problems. A high-protein diet may work well for a breed such as a Labrador Retriever, if you are attempting to guard against obesity, but it does not suit a Weimaraner. This is a high-energy breed, both mentally and physically, and too much protein may result in a dog becoming hyperactive. If you have concerns with regard to diet, consult your vet.

WEIMARANER TANTRUMS

Believe it or not, the Weimaraner can throw as good a tantrum as a two-year-old toddler. In most cases, this applies to a young dog who is challenging your authority. He will protest verbally and may literally dig in his heels and refuse to co-operate. Both males and females throw tantrums, but a female tends to be more excitable and may be more easily wound up.

Just like a human toddler, a Weimaraner will throw a tantrum because he objects to being told what to do. If this happens, you must not become confrontational, as this will only exacerbate the situation. Ideally take your Weimaraner to a safe place, such as his indoor crate, and leave him there so he has a chance to calm down. Leave him for 20 minutes or so, and return as if nothing had happened. Your Weimaraner will have had a chance to change his mind-set, and by taking yourself out of the situation, you have not become the focus of his frustration. Adopt a calm, confident manner, and your Weimaraner will accept your leadership without needing to challenge you further.

DOMINANCE

If you have trained and socialised your Weimaraner correctly, he will know his place in the family pack and will have no desire to challenge your authority. As we have seen, adolescent males test the boundaries, and this is the time to enforce all your earlier training so your Weimaraner accepts that he is not top dog. Weimaraners have a strong protective instinct which can lead to guarding-type behaviour if mismanaged, but ensuring that you remain the pack leader should avoid most problems.

If you have taken on a rescued dog who has not been trained and socialised, or if you have let your adolescent Weimaraner become over-assertive, you may find you have problems with a dominant dog.

Dominance is expressed in many different ways, which may include the following:

- Showing lack of respect for your personal space. For example, your dog will barge through doors ahead of you or jump up at you.
- Getting up on to the sofa or your favourite armchair, and growling when you tell him to get back on the floor.
- Becoming possessive over a toy,

or guarding his food bowl by growling when you get too close.

- Growling when anyone approaches his bed or when anyone gets too close to where he is lying.
- Ignoring basic obedience commands.
- Showing no respect to younger members of the family, pushing amongst them and completely ignoring them.
- Male dogs may start marking (cocking their leg) in the house.
- Aggression towards people. This is a worst-case scenario, and it often starts with a puppy that was allowed to mouth hands or arms and then discovers that a tighter grip has more effect. All signs of mouthing should be censured from a very early age so that your Weimaraner learns, right from the start, that it is entirely unacceptable behaviour.

If you see signs of your Weimaraner becoming too dominant, you must work at lowering his status so that he realises that you are the leader and he must accept your authority. Although you need to be firm, you also need to use positive training methods so that

A Weimaraner who is trying to rule the roost may become possessive over toys.

your Weimaraner is rewarded for the behaviour you want. In this way, his 'correct' behaviour will be strengthened and repeated.

The golden rule is not to confront a Weimaraner when he attempts to assert his authority. For example, a 14-month Weimaraner may have a routine of going for a walk at 10am every morning. One morning you have to go to the dentist, and the walk is delayed until 11am. The unruly Weimaraner will object to the delay by being destructive in your absence. A Weimaraner is never absent-minded in his actions; if he is being destructive, you know there is a reason for it.

In this situation, the best solution is prevention. If you have to change your dog's routine and delay his walk, put him in his indoor crate where he

cannot get up to any mischief. When you return, take your time, and then release your Weimaraner. When you are ready, you can take your Weimaraner for his walk. This has taught him that it is you who dictates his routine, and he must accept your decisions without question. With a Weimaraner, it is all about mind games. If you get the psychology right, your Weimaraner will be content to accept his place in the pecking order.

There are a number of steps you can take to lower your Weimaraner's status. They include:

- Go back to basics and hold daily training sessions. Make sure you have some really tasty treats, or find a toy your Weimaraner really values and only bring it out at training sessions. Run through all the training exercises you have taught your Weimaraner. Make a big fuss of him and reward him when he does well. This will reinforce the message that you are the leader and that it is rewarding to do as you ask.
- Teach your Weimaraner something new; this can be as simple as learning a trick, such as shaking paws. Having something new to think about will mentally stimulate your

Weimaraner, and he will benefit from interacting with you.

- Be 100 per cent consistent with all house rules – your Weimaraner must never sit on the sofa, and you must never allow him to jump up at you.
- If your Weimaraner has been guarding his food bowl, put the bowl down empty, and drop in a little food at a time. Periodically stop dropping in the food, and tell your Weimaraner to "Sit" and "Wait". Give it a few seconds, and then reward him by dropping in more food. This shows your Weimaraner that you are the provider of the food, and he can only eat when you allow him to.
- Make sure the family eats before you feed your Weimaraner. Some trainers advocate eating in front of the dog (maybe just a few bites from a biscuit) before starting a training session, so the dog appreciates your elevated status.
- Do not let your Weimaraner barge through doors ahead of you or leap from the back of the car before you release him. You may need to put your dog on the lead and teach him to "Wait" at doorways, and then reward him for letting you go through first.

If your Weimaraner is progressing well with his retraining programme, think about getting involved with a dog sport, such as agility or competitive obedience. This will give your Weimaraner a positive outlet for his energies. However, if your Weimaraner is still seeking to be dominant, or you have any other concerns, do not delay in seeking the help of an animal behaviourist.

AGGRESSION

Aggression is a complex issue, as there are different causes and the behaviour may be triggered by numerous factors. It may be directed towards people, but far more commonly it is directed towards other dogs. Aggression in dogs may be the result of:

- Dominance (see page 103).
- Defensive behaviour: This may be induced by fear, pain or punishment.
- Territory: A dog may become aggressive if strange dogs or people enter his territory (which is generally seen as the house and garden).
- Intra-sexual issues: This is aggression between sexes – male-to-male or female-to-female.
- Parental instinct: A mother dog may become aggressive if she is protecting her puppies.

A simple exercise, such as teaching your dog to "Wait" so that you go through a doorway first, will strengthen your role as leader.

A dog who has been well socialised (see page 96) and has been given sufficient exposure to other dogs at significant stages of his development will rarely be aggressive. A well-bred Weimaraner that has been reared correctly should not have a hint of aggression in his temperament. If you have established yourself as pack leader in your household, treat your your dog with respect and also insist on your Weimaraner treating you, other humans, and other dogs with respect too, there shouldn't be a problem.

Obviously, if you have taken on an older, rescued dog, you will have little or no knowledge of his background, and if he shows signs of aggression, the cause will need to be determined. In most cases, you would be well advised to call in professional help if you see aggressive behaviour in your dog; if the aggression is directed towards people, you should seek immediate advice. This behaviour can escalate very quickly and could lead to disastrous consequences.

SEPARATION ANXIETY

The Weimaraner should be brought up to accept short periods of separation from his owner so that he does not become anxious. A new puppy should be left for short periods on his own, ideally in a crate where he cannot get up to any mischief. It is a good idea to leave him with a boredom-busting toy (see page 107).

When you return, do not rush to the crate and make a huge fuss. Wait a few minutes, and then calmly go to the crate and release your dog, telling him how good he has been. If this scenario is repeated a number of times, your Weimaraner will soon learn that being left on his own is no big deal.

Problems with separation anxiety are most likely to arise if you take on a rescued dog who has major insecurities. You may also find your Weimaraner hates being left if you have failed to accustom him to short periods of isolation when he was growing up. Separation anxiety is expressed in a number of ways, and all are equally distressing for both dog and owner. An anxious dog who is left alone may bark and whine continuously, urinate and defecate, and may be extremely destructive.

There are a number of steps you can take when attempting to solve this problem.

- Put up a baby-gate between adjoining rooms, and leave your dog in one room while you are in the other room. Your dog will be able to see you and hear you, but he is learning to cope without being right next

A properly educated Weimaraner should be able to tolerate short periods of separation from his owner without becoming stressed. *lynn@kipps.co.uk*

to you. Build up the amount of time you can leave your dog in easy stages.

- Buy some boredom-busting toys (such as kongs) and fill them with some tasty treats. Whenever you leave your dog, give him a food-filled toy so that he is busy while you are away.
- If you have not used a crate before, it is not too late to start. Make sure the crate is big and comfortable, and train your Weimaraner to get used to going in his crate while you are in the same room. Gradually build up the amount of time he spends in the crate, and then start leaving the room for short periods. When you return, do not make a fuss of your dog. Leave him for five or 10 minutes before releasing him so that he gets used to your comings and goings.
- Pretend to go out, putting on your coat and jangling keys, but do not leave the house. An anxious dog often becomes hyped up by the ritual of leave taking, and so this will help to desensitise him.
- When you go out, leave a radio or a TV on. Some dogs are comforted by hearing voices and background noise when they are left alone.
- Try to make your absences as short as possible when you are first training your dog to accept being on his own. When you return, do not fuss your dog, rushing to his crate to release him. Leave him for a few minutes, and, when you go to

You can train your Weimaraner to be a model good citizen.

him, remain calm and relaxed so that he does not become hyped up with a huge greeting.

If you take these steps, your dog should become less anxious, and, over a period of time, you should be able to solve the problem. However, if you are failing to make progress, do not delay in calling in expert help.

NEW CHALLENGES
If you enjoy training your Weimaraner, you may want to try one of the many dog sports that are now on offer.

GOOD CITIZEN SCHEME
This is a scheme run by the Kennel Club in the UK and the American Kennel Club in the USA. The schemes promote

responsible ownership and help you to train a well-behaved dog who will fit in with the community. The schemes are excellent for all pet owners, and they are also a good starting point if you plan to compete with your Weimaraner when he is older. The KC and the AKC schemes vary in format. In the UK there are three levels: bronze, silver and gold, with each test becoming progressively more demanding. In the AKC scheme there is a single test.

Some of the exercises include:

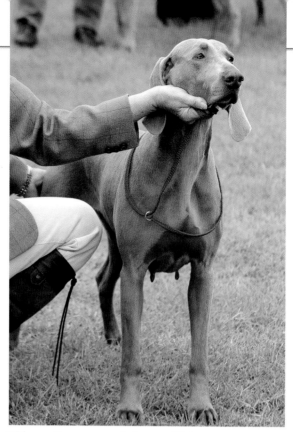

With practice, you can train your Weimaraner to perform in the show ring.

- Walking on a loose lead among people and other dogs.
- Recall amid distractions.
- A controlled greeting where dogs stay under control while their owners meet.
- The dog allows all-over grooming and handling by his owner, and also accepts being handled by the examiner.
- Stays, with the owner in sight, and then out of sight.
- Food manners, allowing the owner to eat without begging, and taking a treat on command.
- Sendaway – sending the dog to his bed.

The tests are designed to show the control you have over your dog, and his ability to respond correctly and remain calm in all situations. The Good Citizen Scheme is taught at most training clubs. For more information, log on to the Kennel Club or AKC website (see Appendices).

THERAPY DOGS

The well-trained Weimaraner is ideally suited to working as a therapy dog; he is gentle, kind and lovable. Therapy dogs go with their owners to visit residents in a variety of different institutions, which may include hospitals, care homes, and prisons. It is widely acknowledged that interacting with a dog has great therapeutic benefits, and so the work is very rewarding. Therapy dogs are assessed to ensure they have the correct temperament, and their owners must have a good measure of control. For more information on training your Weimaraner to be a therapy dog, see Appendices.

SHOWING

In your eyes, your Weimaraner is the most beautiful dog in the world – but would a judge agree? Showing is a highly competitive sport, and only a few dogs ever gain the coveted title of Show Champion.

However, many owners get bitten by the showing bug, and their calendar is governed by the dates of the top showing fixtures.

Many training clubs hold ringcraft classes, which are run by experienced showgoers. At these classes, you will learn how to handle your Weimaraner in the ring, and you will also find out about rules, procedures and show ring etiquette.

The best plan is to start off at some small, informal shows where you can practise and learn the tricks of the trade before graduating to bigger shows. It's a long haul, starting in the very first puppy class, but the dream is to make your Weimaraner up into a Show Champion.

COMPETITIVE OBEDIENCE

Border Collies and German Shepherds dominate this sport, but gundogs have also made their mark at the highest level. The Weimaraner has the intelligence to do well in competitive obedience; the challenge is producing the accuracy that is demanded. The classes start off being relatively easy and become progressively more challenging with additional exercises, and the handler giving minimal instructions to the dog.

Exercises include:

- **Heelwork:** Dog and handler must complete a set pattern on and off the lead, which includes left turns, right turns, about turns, and changes of pace.
- **Recall:** This may be when the handler is stationary or on the move.
- **Retrieve:** This may be a dumbbell or any article chosen by the judge.
- **Sendaway:** The dog is sent to a designated spot and must go into an instant Down until he is recalled by the handler.
- **Stays:** The dog must stay in the Sit and in the Down for a set amount of time. In advanced classes, the handler is out of sight.
- **Scent:** The dog must retrieve a single cloth from a pre-arranged pattern of cloths that has his owner's scent, or, in advanced classes, the judge's scent. There may also be decoy cloths.
- **Distance control:** The dog must execute a series of moves

The athletic Weimaraner shows off his skills competing in agility.

(Sit, Stand, Down) without moving from his position and with the handler at a distance.

Even though competitive obedience requires accuracy and precision, be sure to make it fun for your Weimaraner, with lots of praise and rewards so that you motivate him to do his best.

Many training clubs run advanced classes for those who want to compete in obedience, or you can hire the services of a professional trainer for one-on-one sessions.

AGILITY

This fun sport has grown enormously in popularity over the past few years. If you fancy having a go, make sure you have good control over your Weimaraner and keep him slim. Agility is a very physical sport, which demands fitness from both dog and handler.

In agility competitions, each dog must complete a set course over a series of obstacles, which include:
- Jumps (upright hurdles and long jump)

A close working relationship is essential when competing in field trials.

- Weaves
- A-frame
- Dog walk
- Seesaw
- Tunnels (collapsible and rigid)
- Tyre

Dogs may compete in Jumping classes, with jumps, tunnels and weaves, or in Agility classes, which have the full set of equipment. Faults are awarded for poles down on the jumps, missed contact points on the A-frame, dog walk and seesaw, and refusals. If a dog takes the wrong course, he is eliminated. The winner is the dog that completes the course in the fastest time with no faults. As you progress up the levels, courses become progressively harder with more twists, turns and changes of direction.

If you want to get involved in agility, you will need to find a club that specialises in the sport (see Appendices). You will not be allowed to start training until your Weimaraner is 12 months old, and you cannot compete until he is 18 months old. This rule is for the protection of the dog, who may suffer injury if he puts strain on bones and joints while he is still growing.

FIELD TRIALS

This is a sport where the Weimaraner excels, and a number have been awarded top honours in this discipline.

In field trials, dogs are trained to work in an entirely natural environment. Nothing is set up, staged or artificial. The dogs may be asked to retrieve shot game from any type of terrain, including swamp, thick undergrowth and from water. They also need to perform blind retrieves, where they are sent out to find shot game when they haven't seen it fall. Dogs are judged on their natural game-finding abilities, their work in the shooting field, and their response to their handler. The two most crucial elements are steadiness and obedience.

The Weimaraner's original role was to work in the field, so it is not surprising that he is able to perform particularly well. One of the Weimaraner's primary characteristics – his ability to think for himself – lends itself ideally to success in field trials and as a working gundog.

The other great plus factor is that Weimaraners love to work closely with their handlers, so, if you put in the training, you could get to the top levels and even make your Weimaraner into a Field Trial Champion.

If you are not aiming for the dizzy heights of making up a Field Trial Champion, you can test your Weimaraner's working ability with the Gundog Working Certificate, which examines basic hunting and retrieving skills in the field. If a Show Champion gains a Gundog Working Certificate, he can become a full Champion.

WORKING TRIALS

This is a very challenging sport. It suits some Weimaraners more than others. Weimaraners are highly intelligent but their free-thinking nature means they can become bored by repetition and lose interest. The sport consists of three basic components:

- **Control:** Dog and handler

must complete obedience exercises, but the work does not have to be as precise as it is in competitive obedience. In the advanced classes, manwork (where the dog works as a guard/protection dog) is a major feature.

• **Agility:** The dog must negotiate a 3 ft (0.91 m) hurdle, a 9 ft (2.75 m) long jump, and a 6 ft (1.82) upright scale, which is the most taxing piece of dog equipment.

• **Nosework:** The dog must follow a track that has been laid over a set course. The surface may vary, and the length of time between the track being laid and the dog starting work is increased in the advanced classes.

The ladder of stakes are: Companion Dog, Utility Dog, Working Dog, Tracking Dog and Patrol Dog. In the US, tracking is a sport in its own right, and is very popular among Weimaraner owners.

If you want to get involved in working trials, you will need to find a specialist club or a trainer that specialises in training for working trials. For more information, see Appendices.

The greatest joy of all is simply having fun with your Weimaraner.

FLYBALL
Weimaraners are natural retrievers, so they can be easily trained to be flyball competitors.

Flyball is a team sport; the dogs love it, and it is undoubtedly the noisiest of all the canine sports!

Four dogs are selected to run in a relay race against an opposing team. The dogs are sent out by their handlers to jump four hurdles, catch the ball from the flyball box, and then return over the hurdles. At the top level, this sport is fast and furious, and although it is dominated by Border Collies, the athletic Weimaraner can make a big contribution. This is particularly true in multibreed competitions where the team is made up of four dogs of different breeds, and only one can be a Border Collie or a Working Sheepdog. Points are awarded to dogs and teams. Annual awards are given to top dogs and top teams, and milestone awards are given out to dogs as they attain points

throughout their flyballing careers.

DANCING WITH DOGS
This sport is relatively new, but it is becoming increasingly popular. It is very entertaining to watch, but it is certainly not as simple as it looks. To perform a choreographed routine to music with your Weimaraner demands a huge amount of training.

Dancing with dogs is divided into two categories: heelwork to music and canine freestyle. In heelwork to music, the dog must work closely with his handler and show a variety of close 'heelwork' positions. In canine freestyle, the routine can be more flamboyant, with the dog working at a distance from the handler and performing spectacular tricks. Routines are judged on style and presentation, content and accuracy.

SUMMING UP
The Weimaraner is a popular companion dog, and deservedly so. He is intelligent, fun-loving and loyal. Make sure you keep your half of the bargain: spend time socialising and training your Weimaraner so that you can be proud to take him anywhere and he will always be a credit to you.

THE PERFECT WEIMARANER

Chapter 7

A Breed Standard is a blueprint of the perfect dog to which fanciers of that breed adhere. It is useful to all who love the breed and want to promote it successfully. The Standard was laid down in this precise way because a dog of this construction, size, colour and temperament would fulfil the needs of the fancier. The Weimaraner has indeed done this for centuries, before being recognised officially as a breed in 1896. We, the breed's present-day custodians, owe it to our Weimaraners not to change them just to follow the fashion of the day. All too often this has happened with other breeds, frequently with devastating results and consequent breathing, hereditary and whelping problems. We can and must continue to learn from this in order to keep our breed sound.

Before breeding or judging you must understand the basic construction of dogs and have a thorough knowledge of the pertinent Breed Standard. It is essential that the Standard is interpreted properly. For example, all too often I read in so-called judges' critiques the words 'pale colour' relating to the Weimaraner's coat colour, yet in no Standard I have read is the word 'pale' used.

Personal preferences mean that not everyone will interpret the Standard in precisely the same way. This is good, because these preferences usually balance out and the end result is that breeders are aware of different aspects of the Standard. In fact, this has happened with breeders of the Weimaraner in the UK, who have bred with their eyes open. This has resulted in the Weimaraner being, at present, one of the soundest breeds in construction in the gundog group.

GOVERNING BODIES OF THE BREED STANDARD

The Weimaraner has three governing bodies covering the Breed Standard. The Fédération Cynologique Internationale (FCI), which has 80 member countries, adopted the German Standard, as this is the country of origin, and this was last revised in 1990. The American Kennel Club (AKC) Standard was revised in 1972 and the Kennel Club in Britain (KC) revised its Standard in 1987.

In 1953 The Weimaraner Club of Great Britain was formed, with Major Petty as its first secretary. The club translated the German Standard when the breed was first introduced, but the Kennel Club's 1987 revision was shorter and more to the point, in accordance with the wishes of the parent club and its many advisors.

This is essentially a working gundog, presenting a picture of power, stamina and balance. The Weimaraner pictured is Sh. Ch. Flimmoric Fanclub.

'Medium' is a word covering the Weimaraner. The dog should be balanced throughout, each part fitting in harmony with the next, presenting a total animal that can work all day, hunting, galloping, jumping and carrying heavy birds or game. If, for instance, the forequarters are overdone, pressure on bones, muscles and vital organs results, shortening the efficiency of the animal and ultimately the dog's life. In the shooting field you often see the most unsound, unbalanced specimens of certain breeds of gundogs, yet work they do – and extremely well. However, the things keeping such an animal going more than anything are desire, instinct, and a big heart.

When breeding we should do the best for our chosen breed and try to produce a dog that can live a long, pain-free life to the full. If I were to equate a dog to a horse, the Weimaraner is the canine equivalent of the thoroughbred: athletic, powerful, muscular – and a breathtaking sight when galloping.

Basically, all three Standards are very similar. The UK Breed Standard is possibly more open to wrong interpretation by being less specific. The German Standard has the greatest differences from the British and American Standards.

INTERPRETATION AND ANALYSIS

GENERAL APPEARANCE

KC
Medium sized, grey with light eyes. Presents a picture of power, stamina and balance.

AKC
A medium sized gray dog, with fine aristocratic features. He should present a picture of grace, speed, stamina, alertness and balance. Above all, the dog's conformation must indicate the ability to work with great speed and endurance in the field.

FCI
A medium large to large gundog. Effectively a working type, elegant, sinewy, with a powerful muscular system. The male and female sex must be clearly defined.

TEMPERAMENT, BEHAVIOUR, CHARACTER

KC
Fearless, friendly, protective, obedient and alert. Hunting ability of paramount concern.

AKC
The temperament should be friendly, fearless, alert and obedient.

The versatile Weimaraner thrives on being given the opportunity to use his brains and his body.

David Tomlinson

FCI

A versatile, easy-going, fearless and enthusiastic gundog with a systematic and persevering search, yet not excessively fast. A remarkably good nose. Sharp on prey and game. Also man-sharp, yet not aggressive. Reliable in pointing and waterwork. Remarkable inclination to work after the shot.

All three Standards stress that a Weimaraner should have working ability. In an ideal world all Weimaraners would be shot over in one capacity or another — but then, in an ideal world, I would not have to work! Whether you want a Weimaraner to work or not, that instinct is still, and

should still, be there. It is wonderful to watch. When out walking, your Weimaraner will quarter, even in the park, and many Weimaraners will go rigid on point, even on an old discarded tennis ball, lost in undergrowth. I have proudly been presented with a slimy decaying skeleton of a bird, for which I have been truly grateful, on more than one occasion!

However, the Weimaraner makes a wonderful pet/companion and an enjoyable dog should you want to compete in working trials or agility. And many people show their Weimaraners with great success. So this versatile breed lends itself to many facets. A priority when owning a Weimaraner is to

provide stimulation. When reproducing the Weimaraner, in our endeavour to preserve the breed's characteristics, we should certainly only breed from dogs with an instinct to work, and make sure that the puppies are placed into homes that will utilise their inquisitive minds. We are not breeding a lapdog intent on lying in front of the fire all day. I would liken a Weimaraner puppy to a child of higher-than-average intelligence who, if placed in a class of average children, would become bored and probably disruptive, even destructive, due to under-stimulation.

The Standard calls for a friendly, fearless, protective, alert temperament. Bred originally to hunt game such as wild boar and

There should be a distinct difference between the female head (left) and the male head (right). *lynn@kipps.co.uk*

wild cat, the dog needed to be courageous and protective in case such dangerous game turned on its master. Working in thick forests in Weimar, the Weimaraner needed agility and alertness. To have such traits means the dog is brave and quick-thinking, and therefore needs a sound temperament.

This sound temperament should be to the fore in any breeding programme. While the German Standard calls for 'sharp on prey and game', both the American and UK Standards have no mention of such. We require any gundog to be soft-mouthed, able to retrieve game gently so that the master can eat that game. Here in the UK we never want a gundog 'sharp'.

It is often thought that temperament cannot be properly assessed when judging. Gazing into the eye of a horse portrays the soul. So it is with the dog. So much can be read from the expression. The Weimaraner should have a steady gaze, looking back at you honestly, not flighty or nervous, nor with the pupil dilated except in excitement or work.

Likewise the tail carriage sends signals that can be read. A tail clamped down suggests nervousness. Insecurity of temperament in this way is totally unacceptable and leads to biting out of fear. A tail carried high over the back can be a sign of aggression. Watch a terrier on the scent of a rat. The ideal position of the tail should be slightly higher than the level of the back, displaying a confident air. A youngster sometimes carries a

high tail when at the stage of being full of self-importance — a stage that the dog generally grows out of.

HEAD & SKULL

KC
Moderately long, aristocratic; moderate stop, slight median line extending back over forehead. Rather prominent occipital bone. Measurement from top of nose to stop equal to measurement from stop to occipital prominence. Flews moderately deep, enclosing powerful jaw. Foreface straight, delicate nostrils. Skin tightly drawn. Nose grey.

AKC
Moderately long and aristocratic, with moderate stop and slight median line extending back over the forehead. Rather prominent occipital bone and trumpets well set back, beginning at the back of the eye-sockets. Measurement from tip of nose to stop equal to that from stop to occipital bone. The flews should be straight, delicate at the nostrils. Skin drawn tightly. Neck clean-cut and moderately long. Expression kind, keen and intelligent. Nose gray.

FCI
In proportion to the body size and with the facial structure in the dog broader than with the bitch, yet with both in good proportion in relation to the width of the top of the head

and the total length of the head. On the centre of the forehead a groove. Occiput lightly to moderately protruding. Behind the eyes clearly visible cheek bone. Forehead area (Stop) extremely small.
Nose sponge large, pointing over the lower jaw, dark flesh-coloured, receding gradually changing to grey. Ridge straight, frequently a little raised, never dished.

Although the head in a male is altogether bigger than in a bitch, neither of them should be coarse. There should be width of skull to allow for brain room (but the skull should not be domed), with the median line across the skull from occiput to stop being slightly lighter in colour on the head. The length from stop, and stop to nose, is equal. This, coupled with the fact that the nose to stop should not be dished, and may even be very slightly raised, contributes to the snooty, aristocratic expression. The cheeks should be clean, not wide or fleshy. The flews or top lip should cover a powerful jaw, without being pendulous or deep; nor should they be snipey or go to a point, drawing tight over the jaw.
   Scent is taken by the nostril and therefore the nose should be large with open nostrils, yet not bulbous. The nose is grey – not black, as in many breeds. Heads develop at different times during maturity and can often appear unbalanced. A snipey head rarely develops into anything different.

The skull is broad and the ears are set on high.   *David Tomlinson*

A broad, coarse head will rarely change either, yet a doggy head on a bitch, and a bitch head on a dog, will generally even out beautifully in a mature animal. Likewise a bitch with a plain head will often mature and develop following a season, as will the bitch generally.

EARS

KC
Long and lobular, slightly folded and set high. When drawn alongside jaw, should end approximately 1 inch from the point of the nose.

AKC
Long and lobular, slightly folded and set high. The ear when drawn snugly alongside the jaw should end

approximately two inches from the point of the nose.

FCI
Broad and fairly long, reaching to about the corner of the mouth. High and narrow at the inset, rounded off into a point at the bottom. When alert, turned slightly forwards, folds.

The ears are set on high, which goes with the broad flat skull. The domed skull tends to go with the low-set ear, as in setters. The ear leather is fine. I tend to notice that any dog with a thick leather may be inclined to be coarse. The fine, long ear (finishing to within an inch of the nose, when held down towards the jaw) has a distinctive fold. The character of this fold is more important than the actual length

The piercing blue eyes of a puppy.   *lynn@kipps.co.uk*

With maturity, the eyes become amber in colour.

of the ear, so the difference between the Standards is not particularly important. In a young puppy the ear appears particularly long — imagination suggests that your puppy, at about 18 weeks of age, is about to take off and fly when running towards you with flapping ears. While Weimaraners do not often suffer from ear problems, they do often catch their ears, which then bleed profusely and end up with scars and bits missing.

EYES

KC
Medium sized. Shades of amber or blue grey. Placed far enough apart to indicate good disposition, not too protruding or deeply set. Expression keen, kind and intelligent.

AKC
In shades of light amber, gray or blue gray, set well enough apart to indicate good disposition and intelligence. When dilated under excitement the eyes may appear almost black.

FCI
Amber coloured, dark to light with an intelligent expression. In puppy stage sky blue. Round, hardly slanted. Eyelids flat (well-fitting showing no haw).

The colour is quite unique, being a piercing blue in a youngster under about 18 months, turning to amber with maturity. The eyes should be round, well-set, not too deep, giving a piggy appearance, nor bulbous, which could cause health problems. The skin around the eye should be close-fitting, showing no red, loose haw. Otherwise this could be problematic. The eyes should be set not too close together, nor too wide, but looking forward with that characteristic, aristocratic look.

MOUTH/TEETH

KC
Jaws strong with a perfect regular and complete scissors bite, i.e. upper teeth closely overlapping lower teeth and set square to the jaws. Lips and gums of pinkish, flesh colour. Complete dentition highly desirable.

AKC
Teeth well set, strong and even,

well-developed and proportionate to jaw with correct scissors bite, the upper teeth protruding slightly over the lower teeth but not more than 1/16th of an inch. Complete dentition is greatly to be desired. Lips and gums pinkish flesh shades.

FCI

Complete, regular and strong. Cutting teeth moving in a grating fashion (scissor bite). Jaw powerful. Lips moderately overhanging, flesh coloured with a small fold at the corner of the mouth. Cheeks muscular and clearly formed. 'Dry head'. Muzzle long and, especially with the dog, strong in profile, working almost to a right angle.

The Weimaraner, being a retrieving breed, needs a strong jaw and complete dentition with a scissor bite. This means that the front teeth close with the top teeth slightly over the bottom teeth. If the gap is too great, this is overshot and, in a youngster, I prefer to see a slightly overshot mouth, as the bottom jaw grows at a different rate, thus catching up and producing the correct mouth in an adult. An undershot jaw is when the bottom teeth protrude in front of the top. A wry mouth is when the jaw is slightly twisted. When breeding, mouths should always be considered. If a dog with a bad mouth is bred from, the problem is difficult to breed out and we must remember that the mouth is important to a dog whose job includes retrieving.

NECK

KC and AKC

Clean cut and moderately long.

FCI

Of noble appearance and stately. Upper profile curved, muscular, nearly round, with a good reach and dry. Getting stronger towards the shoulder and harmoniously merging into the back line and chest.

The neck supports the dog when carrying heavy game, often over obstacles and uneven terrain, so it must be muscular and strong. Too long and the neck loses strength, too short and the neck is cloddy, making picking game and scenting much harder work. The neck needs to be 'dry' or 'clean', without dewlap or loose hanging skin, except in a youngster, which often appears to be wearing an older dog's skin by mistake. The neck should fit neatly into the shoulders; this will be the case if the shoulders are correctly angulated.

FOREQUARTERS

KC

Forelegs straight and strong. Measurement from elbow to ground equal to distance from elbow to top of withers.

AKC

Straight and strong, with the measurement from the elbow to the ground approximately equalling the distance from the elbow to the top of the withers.

The teeth meet in a scissor bite with the teeth on the upper jaw closely overlapping the teeth on the lower jaw.

FCI

Forelegs: Generally legs 'high', sinewy, straight and parallel, but not broad standing (too wide).
Shoulders: Long and sloping, well (close) fitting, strongly muscular. Good angulation of the shoulder blade over arm 'hinge' (where shoulder joins to the withers).
Upper Arm: Set at a slant, long enough and strong (from point) of shoulder to elbows.
Elbows: Free and straight set. Neither turned inwardly nor outwardly.
Under Arm: Long, positioned straight.
Pastern Joint: Powerful, tight.
Pastern: Sinewy, slightly slanting.

FOREQUARTERS

When viewed from the front, the forelegs are straight and strong.
lynn@kipps.co.uk

The shoulders must be properly constructed in order to carry the weight of the forequarters.
lynn@kipps.co.uk

The forelegs should be straight when viewed from the front, not bowed. The bone must be strong, not fine and weak, nor coarse, making the dog cloddy and clumsy. Neither should the feet turn inwards, which can be a sign of bad shoulder placement or over-knuckling when the pastern is too straight. Nor should the feet turn out, east and west, which is a sign of weak pasterns. The movement accompanying this is that the dog throws out and flaps the front feet when moving. Sometimes an unbalanced youngster stands east and west, but this rights itself as the dog grows and strengthens. If an older dog stands east-west, this shows a lack of exercise, or a construction fault, and would be penalised.

The pasterns, while not being weak, should have 'give' in them. If you think of the pastern as the shock-absorber, if it is too straight then jarring will occur when the dog is moving and jumping. If weak, the pasterns will possibly let the dog down, especially with age. If front legs appear to be close together, the dog lacks forechest, which a Weimaraner needs, coupled with spring of rib and length of rib cage. In this area the engine of this galloping breed is contained, and room is required so the lungs can function properly and there is heart room.

The greatest weight is carried by the forequarters, so shoulders should be properly constructed. We require well-laid shoulder blades, coupled with good length of upper arm. Although an exact angle is not defined, it is generally accepted that an angle of 90 degrees is correct. This gives enough leverage of foreleg, which means the dog has good front extension when moving. If the shoulder blade is not laid correctly, the upper arm is short and the dog can only move forward by the legs being lifted in hackney action, putting more wear on the dog's front assembly and using more energy. The shoulder blade will be wide at the withers. This can also have the effect of making the dog wide at the elbow, again obstructing free movement. When standing naturally, or 'stacked' for the show ring, the side view of the front assembly shows the shoulder placement and good front if the dog's elbow is in a straight line up to the withers.

The Weimaraner is noted for its length of body.   lynn@kipps.co.uk

BODY

KC
Length of body measured from highest point of withers to ground. Topline level, with slightly sloping croup. Chest well developed, deep. Shoulders well laid. Ribs well sprung, ribcage extending well back. Abdomen firmly held, moderately tucked up flank. Brisket should drop to elbow.

AKC
The back should be moderate in length, set in a straight line, strong and should slope slightly from the withers. The chest should be well developed and deep with shoulders well laid back. Ribs well sprung and long. Abdomen firmly held;

moderately tucked up flank. The brisket should extend to the elbow.

FCI
Topline: From the curved neck line over the well-formed wither harmoniously merging into the relatively long, strong back.
Wither: Clearly defined.
Back: Strong and muscular, without hollow. At the back not over built. (High behind.) A slightly longer back, as it is characteristic to the breed, is not faulty.
Croup: Pelvis long and with a moderate slope.
Chest: Powerful, but not too wide, with enough depth, nearly reaching the elbows and sufficiently long. Good curve, without being barrel shaped (long chest).
Belly-Line: Slightly increasing,

however belly not showing. Clearly defined flank. (Area below loin.)

PROPORTIONS

FCI
Body length to wither height about 12:11. Length proportions of the head, from the tip of the nose to the start of the forehead slightly longer than from there to the occipital bone. Front legs, length from elbows to the middle of front middle foot knuckles, and length from elbows to withers, about the same.

The body of the Weimaraner is long in comparison to many breeds. Before judges understood the breed properly, many Weimaraners were penalised for being too long. All dogs have 13

HINDQUARTERS

The hindquarters are muscular and well developed.

lynn@kipps.co.uk

The angulation of the stifle should be in harmony with the angulation of the shoulder.

lynn@kipps.co.uk

pairs of ribs. In a shorter-backed dog the ribs do not extend as far back as in a long-backed dog. Either way, no dog requires a long loin. The loin should be well muscled, giving support to the vertebrae, as this is the 'weak link' in the spine. Because there is no support over the loin, other than muscle, the loin should be approximately the length of a hand span, so retaining strength. The ribs support the vertebrae. Ribs should be well sprung, rounded and deep, not too round or barrel-ribbed, which often goes hand in hand with a shallow body — the ribs not reaching the elbow. This will not give room for the lungs and heart, which is needed in this galloping breed. Weimaraners need this forechest and a hand-width between the front legs – again to allow heart and lung room.

A moderate tuck-up means that the abdomen is firmly held but not pulled up, as with a Greyhound or Whippet. Insufficient tuck-up can also appear when the animal is dipped in the topline. The topline will be level to the croup, which is slightly sloping, giving a slightly lower tail-set than many breeds. When judging a Weimaraner the construction can generally be seen. The reason why hands are laid over the ribs, loin and hindquarters is to feel the quality of muscle or, indeed, fat. A Weimaraner should have hard muscle, not fat.

HINDQUARTERS

KC

Moderately angulated, with well-turned stifle. Hocks well let down, turned neither in nor out. Musculation well developed.

AKC

Well angulated stifles and straight hocks. Musculation well developed.

FCI

Hindlegs: Generally legs 'high', sinewy, muscular, parallel in placing, not turned outwardly nor inwardly.
Upper Thigh: Of sufficient length, strong and muscular.
Stifle joint: Powerful and tight.
'Under Leg' (from stifle joint to hock joint): Long tendons clearly protruding.
Hock Joint: Powerful and tight.
Hind Middle Foot: (Hock joint to pad.) Sinewy, nearly vertically placed.

'Moderately angulated' is required in the UK Standard. The USA Standard calls for 'well angulated' stifles. This could lead to a different interpretation of the original meaning and, when shown, there is a very different way of stacking the Weimaraner in each country. In the UK we stack the Weimaraner with a level topline and therefore moderately angulated hindquarters. In the USA the hindquarters are stood further back from the body, giving a sloping topline and a much more angulated appearance to the quarters. If stood naturally, the animal will not stand as angulated and the actual type of Weimaraner does not differ as much as one would assume when looking at photographs. Over-angulation can lead to the animal being cow-hocked. The thing we do strive for is balance. Exaggeration leads to weakness and strain on other parts, which have to compensate for the weakness.

The angle of the bend of stifle is in sympathy with the shoulder angulation, thus producing correct movement where hind legs follow in the path of the front legs. If there is over-angulation in the hindlegs, the dog, when moving, can only 'crab' – move with the hindlegs going to the side – because they go faster than the front legs or 'run up behind', which forces the topline to be higher than the rear. Any movement other than the desired leads to an imbalance, putting pressure on certain parts. The tibia should be of good length to allow the hock to be 'well let down' or lower to the ground. This gives moving power, which produces better drive.

Just as the forequarters need to be soundly constructed because they carry the greatest weight of the dog, so the hindquarters need to be correct because they produce drive and lift, giving this hunting, retrieving breed the power to do its job. It is therefore very necessary for the dog to have good width and quantity of muscle. When viewed from the side, the width of second thigh shows between the hock and stifle joint. This should be full and wide. Above this the thigh muscle should also be full, with good density of muscle, not soft and spongy. Poor-quality muscle is due

to lack of exercise, which is abhorrent in an active gundog such as the Weimaraner.

When viewed from behind, the dog should have wide, full buttocks, and the hocks should be parallel to the floor (not cow-hocked or bowing – again, a weakness). If the hip bones are narrow and muscle poor, often the dog moves close behind. I have also noticed that a young puppy can have super quarters, yet with over-exercise in a growing youngster (under one year old), this can lead to weakness and narrow quarters in an adult. We would not allow a 12-year-old human to run in a marathon — neither should we walk a young dog's legs off. The Weimaraner has a big heart coupled with the desire to go, and will run as long as you allow, without appearing tired. So be patient: refrain from heavy exercise until you have an adult.

FEET

KC
Firm, compact. Toes well arched, pads close, thick. Nails short, grey or amber in colour. Dewclaws customarily removed.

AKC
Firm and compact, webbed, toes well-arched, pads closed and thick, nails short and gray or amber in color. Dewclaws should be removed.

FCI
Front Feet: Closed and powerful. Standing straight to body centre. Toes arched. Longer middle toes are characteristic to the breed so consequently not faulty. Claws light to dark grey. Pads well-pigmented, coarse. Hind Feet: Closed and powerful, without dewclaws, otherwise like front feet.

STRUCTURE OF THE FEET

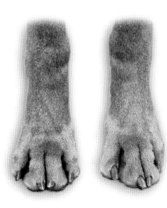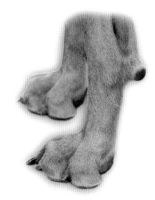

The Weimaraner should have tight, arched feet. *lynn@kipps.co.uk*

Regardless of whether the tail is docked or not, it should be carried in such a way that it denotes confidence.   *lynn@kipps.co.uk*

While a Weimaraner requires tight, arched feet, we do not want a round, cat-like foot associated with breeds such as the Golden Retriever. According to the German Standard, longer middle toes are characteristic and could help to give the dog grip. The pads of the foot need to be thick and evenly padded. They cushion the foot and, if correctly proportioned, protect it from thorns and stones.

It is essential that the Weimaraner's nails are kept short, otherwise the foot cannot function correctly. The dewclaws are removed within the first three days of life and can save much pain and distress later, should they be caught in thick undergrowth. The nature of the Weimaraner is brave – and perhaps even a little foolhardy – therefore the chance of the dog damaging an unremoved dewclaw outweighs the minor painless operation of its early excision. Presumably it is for this reason that the English and USA Standards state that the dewclaws are removed.

TAIL

KC

Previously customarily docked. Docked: Customarily docked so that remaining tail covers scrotum in dogs and vulva in bitches. Thickness of tail in proportion to body. Should be carried in a manner expresssing confidence and sound temperament. In longhaired, tip of tail may be removed. Undocked: Moderately set, thickness in proportion to body. Reaching down to hocks and tapering towards the tip. Carried below level of back when relaxed; may be raised when animated. Not curled over back; good hair cover.

AKC

Docked. At maturity it should measure approximately six inches with a tendency to be light rather than heavy and should be carried in a manner expressing confidence and sound temperament. A non-docked tail should be penalized.

FCI

Set of tail slightly deeper under the back line than with other comparable breeds. Tail strong and well covered with hair. In rest position hanging, when alert and in work, horizontal or also carried higher.

Much controversy reigns over the length of the tail – should it be docked or not? The Weimaraner has no undercoat, the undocked tail is unnaturally long and the tail is used in conjunction with working. In thick undergrowth it can be, and frequently is, damaged. Customarily docked (to cover the vulva in bitches), the tail is used to denote temperament, by how it is carried, and where scent is when working. A sound, well-adjusted Weimaraner's tail will be carried at an angle above the body line, denoting confidence. When out, either enjoying a walk or working, you will find the Weimaraner will wag the tail incessantly when taking scent. Whatever your reason for owning this wonderful breed, this instinct is the same and it is fascinating to watch, if only out of curiosity. However, as from April 2007, docking has been banned, by the UK Government, except in dogs whose owners have proved that they will be worked in the field. As such we now have to take the full tail into consideration, which should not be carried over the back or hang down but, as with the Standard of the docked tail, carried in a way denoting confidence.

If a Weimaraner is built correctly, he will move correctly. *lynn@kipps.co.uk*

GAIT/MOVEMENT

KC
Effortless ground covering, indicating smooth co-ordination. Seen from rear, hind feet parallel to front feet. Seen from side, topline remains strong and level.

AKC
The gait should be effortless and should indicate smooth co-ordination. When seen from the rear the hind feet should be parallel to the front feet. When viewed from the side, the topline should remain strong and level.

FCI
Movement sequence in all ways of walking free and flowing.

Hind and front legs placed in a parallel fashion. Gallop long and front. In trot the back stays level. Pacing is undesirable.

The whole construction of these dogs allows them to fulfil their work as early as possible without stress. Therefore if they are made right, they will move right. There is no finer sight than watching these graceful, almost aerodynamically constructed, dogs gallop over a grouse moor or move in unison with their handlers in a show ring, muscles rippling as the light catches, very like a thoroughbred horse performing. We must remember that the whole picture is taken into consideration when assessing a Weimaraner. As the owner of boarding kennels, I see many good movers in the form of crossbreeds, yet they have no type. Having said that, it is important for a gundog to move

with drive from the hindquarters, with reach from well-angulated shoulder placement, therefore giving the big open side gait. The front and hind action are parallel, converging at speed (not crabbing or moving close behind or crossing in front). To assess movement at its best, good training is essential. If a dog trots along, nose to the floor, or jumps at the handler, nothing can be viewed except a disrespectful Weimaraner.

COAT

KC
Smooth, short and sleek. Longhairs from 1 to 2 inches long on body, somewhat longer on neck, chest and belly; tail and back of legs feathered.

AKC
Short, smooth and sleek, solid color.

The body coat of a longhaired Weimaraner is 2.5-5 cms (1-2 ins), with feathering on the tail and the back of the legs.

FCI

Constitution: (a) Shorthaired: short, but longer and denser as with most comparable breeds. Strong, very thick, smooth flat topcoat, with or without a small amount of undercoat. (b) Longhaired: Soft long topcoat with or without undercoat. Flat or a little wavy. Hair at the ear set long and overhanging. At the ear points shorter and velvety. With or without fringing. Hair length on the sides 3-5 cm, under neck, chest and belly usually a little longer. Good feathers and trousers, although at the bottom less long. Tail with good flag. Space between toes hairy. Head hair covering less long. A Sockhaarig (Wirecoat) with medium/long, dense and good-fitting topcoat, thick undercoat and moderately shaped feather and trousers appears occasionally with dogs of mixed breed (undesirable). Skin strong, good, but not too tightly fitting.

This is explained fully in the Standards. Suffice it to say that an animal in peak condition, mentally and physically, usually has a real bloom to the coat. Of course, this will not be the case when the animal is moulting. I notice that Weimaraners who live outside moult more frequently than those 'in house' and weather patterns dictate the moult to a large degree. Because Weimaraners have no undercoat, and therefore no added protection against thorns etc., their coats should be dense to give this protection to the skin. Nevertheless, no judge worth their salt would penalise scars, from tears etc. In fact, I know of a bitch who dived into water to make a retrieve, only to catch herself on an old, discarded wing of a car, ripping her chest and side open. This left a considerable scar, even though she was beautifully stitched by a vet who knew she was shown. She rewarded the vet by gaining her show title!

COLOUR

KC

Preferably silver grey, shades of mouse or roe grey permissible; blending to lighter shade on head and ears. Dark eel stripe frequently occurs along back.

Whole coat gives the appearance of metallic sheen. Small white mark permissible on chest. White spots resulting from injuries not penalised.

AKC

Solid color, in shades of mouse-gray to silver-gray, usually blending to lighter shades on the head and ears. A small white marking on the chest is permitted, but should be penalized on any other portion of the body. White spots resulting from injury should not be penalised. A distinctly blue or black coat is a disqualification.

Silver, roe or mouse grey as well as 'mergers' between these colour tones. Head and ears usually lighter. White markings are only permissible to a small extent on the chest and on the toes. Occasionally over the middle of the back a more or less obvious darker eel stripe. Dogs with clear red-yellow tint can at the most only obtain the score 'good'. Brown tint is a bad fault.

Breeders are striving to preserve the unique colour of the breed.   lynn@kipps.co.uk

We must all strive to preserve the beautiful unique colour of this breed. The coat colour can be varying shades of the basic colour, as the Standard states. We have 20 or so Weimaraners here and they nearly cover the whole range within the Standard. I have noticed not only genetics, but time of year, feeding and housing can lead to different shades of coat colour. However, coat colour can lead to dissension within fanciers of the breed. Some novice enthusiasts will be found to use 'pale' in conjunction with the colour; in fact, 'pale' is defined in the dictionary as 'lacking colour'. What is meant by the inexperienced by the use of this word is that they prefer silver grey — as indeed many enthusiasts do. Funnily enough, only the UK Standard states 'preferred silver grey'. It must be remembered that each point of

the Weimaraner is taken in context. A Weimaraner, even if very dark or muddy coloured, and not ideal in colour, when put on a grouse moor with German Shorthaired Pointers and Vizslas, for instance, will still be identifiable by colour against the other breeds. When the Weimaraner was nicknamed 'The Grey Ghost', it was with good reason. To watch this dog emerge from a mist makes one gasp momentarily at the apparition. When moulting, the coat can appear to have dark 'rain drops' all over the back as the woolly old coat comes out and the new coat takes on a darker shade, which lightens up when the dog has finished moulting. Feeding a small amount of cooking oil and, indeed, massaging the same into a moulting coat, can speed up

the moult, leaving a lovely, shiny, new coat.

The only white allowed on a Weimaraner is a small amount on the chest. Sometimes a Weimaraner may have white 'spurs' (a spot of white behind the pastern) and while it is officially wrong, if the animal is of excellent merit, you will find this usually will not be penalised in the UK. However, in Britain white toes will disqualify dogs from the winning line-up under the majority of judges, as would too much white anywhere else. One point to mention while on the subject of white, is that all puppies will, at some stage, between three months and a year of age, develop white hair on the tail. Many breeders receive calls from alarmed would-be show owners that the beautiful puppy they own has white and cannot therefore be shown. Why the white develops on the tail is a mystery to me. I did think at one time it was a reaction to docking, but I have since noted undocked and longhaired Weimaraners also have the white hair, just in the same place, showing, therefore, that docking is not the cause. The hair will eventually come out, leaving the original grey tail. No judge would penalise this.

An absolute disqualification regarding colour would be if the animal were mismarked —

There is no such thing as a 'perfect dog', but the aim is to breed dogs of quality, which conform as closely as possible to the Breed Standard.

lynn@kipps.co.uk

although there is no disqualification as such in the UK Standard. The Weimaraner who is mismarked displays ginger markings on the legs up to the knee and hock, and would also have distinctive ginger on the muzzle, chin and eyebrows. Under the tail would also be ginger. In fact, the dog looks rather like a washed-out Dobermann. These markings are evident from birth, and will never fade; in fact, they become more prominent. They will not affect the animal's health, but it should not be bred from, as the markings are genetic in origin. The dog's registration will usually be endorsed by the breeder to prevent breeding with the dog, who should never win in a show ring. These markings are thrown up occasionally, although not too often, as responsible breeders avoid doubling up on lines that are known to produce them. It must be remembered that during

a moult or change of coat, a Weimaraner may appear to have ginger bits. These are quite normal and will disappear as the coat is discarded.

SIZE

KC
Height at withers; dogs 61-69cms (24-27 inches). Bitches 56-64cms (22-25 inches).

AKC
Height at the withers: Dogs 25 to 27 inches; Bitches 23 to 25 inches. One inch over or under the specified height of each sex is allowable but should be penalized. Dogs measuring less than 24 inches or more than 28 inches and bitches measuring less than 22 inches or more than 26 inches shall be disqualified.

FCI
Wither height: Dogs 59-70 cm

(23.25-27.5 inches). (Ideal height 61-67 cm, 24- 27 inches). Bitches 57-65 cm (22.5-25.5 inches). (Ideal height 59-63 cm, 23.25-23.75 inches). Weight: Dogs: 30-40 kg (66-88 lbs). Bitches 25-35 kg (55-77 lbs).

It is important that we strive to keep the size of the Weimaraner within the Standard. We all have the capability to produce a puppy on the periphery of the Standard, but we must be careful when breeding. If we breed from such stock, we will increase the chance of the resulting puppies being outside the Standard. Again, the key word is balance. A Weimaraner who is too big will not be able to fulfil any working potential because of undue pressure on bones and organs. Likewise, if too small, the animal would not have the stamina. When breeding from a Weimaraner who is outside, or on the periphery, of the Standard, one should not necessarily use a dog of opposite proportions but look to the pedigree and, if possible, use the knowledge of a more experienced breeder – or do not breed.

SUMMARY
One should try to retain all characteristics of the Weimaraner and objectively interpret the Standard, for the good of the Weimaraner. No dog is perfect, but the great dogs adhere to the Standard of the breed, yet possess an indefinable quality, which will set them apart from the rest.

FAULTS

KC

Any departure from the Standard should be considered a fault and the seriousness with which the fault should be regarded should be in exact proportion to its degree.

Note: Male animals should have two apparently normal testicles fully descended into the scrotum.

AKC

Tail too short or too long. Pink nose.

FCI

All deviations from the above mentioned points can be seen as a fault. The judgement of them is in exact relation to the extent of the deviation.

1. Distinct deviation in type. Sex uncharacteristic.
2. Large deviations in the proportions.
3. Slight character flaws.
4.1. Large deviations in size and proportions.
4.2. Facial structure. Large deviations e.g. lips too thick, shorter or snipey muzzle.
4.3. Jaw and teeth missing more than 2 P1 or M3.
4.4. Eyes. Slight lid defects, especially when also one-sided.
4.5. Ears. Really short or long, not folded.
5. Throat. Large deviations in shape and muscle.
6. Back. Sway or roach backed, overbuilt.
6.1. Chest and Belly. Barrel-shaped ribs, insufficient chest depth or length, pulled up belly, too much tuck.
6.2. Sex Organs. Clear deviations in the shape, size or consistency of testicles.
7.1. Limbs. Large positional anomalies e.g. poor angles, outwardly turned elbows.
7.2. Hind Limbs. Marked 0-shaped legs or cow hocks.
8. Poor movement in individual ways of walking. Also faulty 'forestep' or 'forehove' — 'stepwalk' (pacing).
9. Coat. Big inadequacies e.g. coat very fine or very coarse.

MAJOR FAULTS

AKC

Doggy bitches. Bitchy dogs. Improper muscular condition. Badly affected teeth. More than four teeth missing. Back too long or too short. Faulty coat. Neck too short, thick or throaty. Low set tail. Elbows in or out. Feet east or west. Poor gait. Poor feet. Cow hocks. Faulty backs either roached or sway. Badly overshot, or undershot bite. Snipey muzzle. Short ears.

DISQUALIFYING FAULTS

AKC

Deviation in height of more than one inch from the Standard either way. A distinctly long coat. A distinctly blue or black coat.

FCI

- Totally untypical, above all clumsy or weak.
- Totally unproportioned.
- Character flaws e.g. timid or frightened.
- Totally untypical e.g. Bulldog-like top of head.
- Absolutely untypical e.g. dished face
- Overshot, undershot, further teeth missing.
- Entropion and ectropion.

HAPPY AND HEALTHY

Chapter 8

The Weimaraner's keen nose and tracking ability make him ideal for other purposes, as well as hunting. As a house dog the Weimaraner will enjoy life more if he is given plenty of exercise and a chance for mental stimulation through different activities. In order to keep your Weimaraner healthy, you must provide him with stimulating walks, as well as feeding a balanced diet and taking veterinary care with necessary vaccinations and parasite control.

Visits to the veterinary surgeon are required for vaccinations, at which time it is usual to make a physical examination of the dog for any undisclosed disease. In between times, daily grooming of the dog will help you to get to know the dog's coat and the body structure, so that signs of illness can be detected earlier than if left until the dog is in pain or refusing his food. Improved diet and routine vaccinations are contributing to a much longer life for all domestic animals, but the owner of the dog has a role to play in everyday health care, too.

It is very important that you really get to know your dog, as you will more easily identify when the dog is 'off colour'. You should then be able to decide whether the dog needs rest, or to be taken to the veterinary surgery. It is also important to know the signs of a healthy dog when you go to buy a puppy. Visits to the vet should be made when some abnormality is detected. Claiming on pet insurance has provided the opportunity for extensive tests and procedures to be undertaken on dogs, but it is important to make an assessment of what each policy will offer and what sort of limits are put on expense, age limit or hereditary disorders requiring veterinary attention before purchasing a policy.

VACCINATIONS

It is best to take all available measures to keep your Weimaraner healthy; one of the greatest advances in canine practice in the last 50 years has been the development of effective vaccines to prevent diseases. Within living memory, dogs died from fits after distemper virus infections; and in the last 20 years many puppies have contracted parvovirus, which, in the early years, often proved to be fatal.

The routine use of a multiple component vaccine to protect against canine distemper, infectious canine hepatitis, parvovirus and Leptospirosis is accepted; but there are still local differences in the age when the puppy receives his first injection or 'shot'. The timing for the primary vaccine course is based

It is essential for puppies to be vaccinated against the major contagious diseases. *lynn@kipps.co.uk*

WORMING & PARASITE CONTROL

Routine worming every three months is essential in order to reduce the risk of infection of susceptible humans handling the dog. Dewormers are necessary for puppies as well as for adult dogs. Many puppies are infested with roundworms, but some breeders will start worming the pregnant bitch to reduce the risk to the newborn pups. Worming of the puppy from two weeks of age, repeated at regular intervals, is advised. Roundworms, hookworms, tapeworms and whipworms present different threats, while heartworms, which can result from the bite of an infected mosquito, are a particular problem of the southeast Atlantic and Gulf Coasts of the USA. This is another parasite to consider if you are planning to take your dog to mainland Europe, as heartworm is endemic from the Mediterranean area of France southwards.

Fleas used to be the greatest problem for dog owners, since not only do they bite humans, but a single flea on the dog's coat can cause persistent scratching and restlessness. Many effective anti-flea preparations are now available – some as tablets by mouth, some as coat applications and some as residual sprays to apply to carpets and upholstery frequented by cats as well as dogs. Lice, fleas, Cheyletiella, mites that burrow under the skin and mites on the surface may all cause disease and are not easily recognised by the eye, but ticks

on an understanding of when the immunity provided by the mother declines to a level that will not interfere with the immune response. Canine vaccines currently in use in the UK have recommendations for the final dose of the primary course to be given at 10 or 12 weeks of age, with boosters after the first year. With the gundog breeds this annual dose is especially necessary for protection against potentially fatal Leptospira, which occur in water and where rats have been present. The length of protection provided after two injections for the puppy is not significantly greater than 12 months (challenges after this date results in shedding of Leptospires) and for some vaccines it is considered less than 12 months. For the other protection against the viruses, a minimum of three years is possible and here annual boosters are less essential. In the

way of things not all animals would be unprotected, so further booster vaccination is recommended at intervals decided by the vet with a local knowledge to protect any of those individual dogs who may have low or marginal blood level titres.

Protection against kennel cough, a distressing infectious disease, is advised, as it is usually acquired from airborne contact with other dogs, especially those stressed when visiting dog shows or boarding kennels. There are several vaccines available and, again, advice should be obtained from your vet as to which type of protection is appropriate to the dog's exposure.

A rabies vaccine is necessary for all dogs leaving the United Kingdom, but it is routine in many countries, as is the vaccine for Lyme disease in the USA, where it should be discussed with the veterinarian.

become large and visible as they gorge themselves with the dog's blood. A thorough grooming of the dog each day will detect many of these parasites; apply suitable preventive products as needed. These may be supplied as a powder, a shampoo, a spot-on insecticide or spray. The active ingredient in insecticides (such as organophosphate or carbamate) are not toxic to humans since these have been substituted by the safer synthetic pyrethroids, phenylpyrazole (fipronil), or avermectin (selamectin).

Spot-on treatment is effective in eliminating external parasites.

DIET AND EXERCISE FOR HEALTH

Some dogs are naturally lean and are perfectly fit, even though they appear to carry little body fat. It is a good idea to weigh all dogs on a regular basis; the dog that appears thin but still actively fit has fewer reserves to fall back on, and weighing on a weekly basis can detect further weight loss before any disastrous change can occur. Each dog should have an ideal weight, and, within a narrow range, the actual correct weight for the dog will act as a guide. Keep records of the dog's weight including the normal weight, the weight lost or gained, and specific diet details.

COAT, EARS AND FEET

The Weimaraner's coat should be short, smooth and sleek, while the longhaired Weimaraner coat is thicker and more waterproof. Too much confinement indoors with warm room temperatures can lead to loss of hair density for outdoor protection. Regular brushing and grooming stimulates the skin and provides an opportunity for close inspection of the underlying skin; these regular checks for traces of fleas or ticks attached to the skin can prevent itching and hair loss. The condition of the skin and hair contributes to the dog's overall health. Grooming stimulates the hair growth stage, known as anagen, by the removal of dead, shedding hairs. This helps to prevent bareness or bald patches. The removal of any eye or other discharge prevents coat matting and skin irritation.

During grooming, daily care and attention to any bony prominences, skin folds, feet and claws, eyes and ears, mouth and teeth, anus, vulva and prepuce also help to keep the dog healthy and identify any potential problems. When grooming the dog, always make a point of checking the ears both inside and out. There may often be a slightly sweet smell, but as soon as ear problems occur, the aroma becomes very pungent. The start of ear trouble can also be detected by the way the dog holds his head.

Lip folds should be checked for saliva soaking or unpleasant breath smells. You may need to wash your Weimaraner in order to eradicate and control ectoparasites or to cleanse the coat and remove smells. Bathing is also often used to improve the appearance of the coat before a show.

The pads of the feet should feel quite soft to touch and not leathery or horny (hyperkeratinised). The pigment of the foot pads is often similar to the nose colour. Between the toes is a hairy area of skin that contains sebaceous glands used for scent marking; sometimes cysts and swellings develop if the glands become blocked. The skin

Keep a close check on your Weimaraner so you can spot any signs of trouble at an early stage.

between the toes is very sensitive to chemical burns and some alkaline clay soils will provoke inflammation with lameness known as 'pedal eczema'. If the dog is not exercised on a hard surface, nail trimming may be required as part of the regular care of the dog's feet, being especially careful to avoid hurting the dog by cutting into the quick. The nails should be of even length and not split at the ends after being left to grow too long. Giving a titbit after the pedicure encourages the dog to accept the procedure.

A TO Z OF COMMON AILMENTS

ALLERGIES

Allergies are now a common diagnosis for many dogs with skin or intestinal disorders. Unlike humans, there is no easy way to demonstrate a food allergy in animals. Younger dogs may develop swelling on the lips, muzzle and eyelids. If very itchy, veterinary treatment is advised. A process of eliminating possible antigens in the diet or in the environment may eventually help to find a cause and there are commercial diets available that may help. If a particular protein causing the allergy is found, it should be eradicated, but often medication can be used to suppress the allergic response; both antihistamines and steroids may be tried when a suitable treatment regime is found.

ANAEMIA

This is a condition where there is not enough haemoglobin to carry oxygen by the blood or where there are insufficient red blood cells. It can only be diagnosed after the examination of the dog's blood. Veterinary examinations usually involving blood tests will help to find the cause of the anaemia and the most appropriate treatment. It was once thought that a lack of dark pigment on the nose was a sign of anaemia, but there is no evidence to show that giving an 'iron tonic' has any benefit to such dogs.

ANAL DISORDERS – ANAL SACCULITIS, TUMOURS: ADENOMATA

Modern diets are often blamed for the high incidence of dogs needing their anal 'glands' squeezed out at regular intervals. These glands are actually little sacs just at the edge of the anus opening and contain strong-smelling, greasy substances used to 'mark' freshly passed faeces for other animals to recognise. Over-production of the fluid causes the dog discomfort, and, when a suitable floor surface is available, the dog will then 'scoot' along, leaving a trail of odorous matter. Occasionally, infection of the gland will alter the smell and this may result in other dogs being attracted to a female type odour; a course of antibiotics can have a direct benefit on this apparent behaviour problem.

Abscesses of the anal sacs are very painful, and may require drainage, although they often swell and burst on their own, with a sudden blood-stained discharge; flushing out and antibiotics may be required as treatment. Other glands around the anus may become cancerous and attention is drawn to these if they start to bleed.

Adenomata are tumours found in the older male dog and require veterinary attention before bleeding occurs.

ARTHRITIS

This joint disease was once often found after an infection, but now the condition is usually either due to joint wear and tear (degenerative) or as a result of an immune system reaction – for example, rheumatoid arthritis and idiopathic arthritis. At first, degenerative arthritis improves with exercise, but later, the dog will stiffen and, on bending the joint, often a painful, grating 'crepitus' can be found. Treatment is aimed at keeping the dog mobile, any excess weight should be lost, and anti-inflammatory medication on a daily basis will remove pain and discomfort. Blood tests and X-rays may be needed for investigating the arthritis. Some owners have

good results using supplements such as the glycosaminoglycans.

ATOPIC DERMATITIS

This skin disorder is found in dogs with an inherited disposition to inflammatory and itching skin disease; characteristically, these signs develop in the first years of life. Secondary bacterial infection or fungal infections may develop in about a third of affected dogs, after the licking and scratching of the affected parts of the body that have less resistance to the normal skin bacteria and Malassezia fungus present on the body.

The immunity to allergens in the environment is low. Shorthaired breeds may be more susceptible than some others, as there is no dense coat cover to keep irritants from the skin. Roughened, itchy, oozing skin may be caused by the immune reactions to various allergens, such as fleas or pollen. There is often a seasonal change if specific pollens are the cause.

AURAL HAEMATOMA

The sudden swelling of the earflap, due to internal bleeding between the skin and the ear cartilage, can be distressing to the Weimaraner and will cause repeated head shaking. Bleeding is

usually the result of fierce scratching with the hind toes, perhaps triggered by a tingling inside the ear canal. Grass seeds or other foreign bodies entering the tube of the outer ear will also provoke such scratching. Ear mites acquired from cats can have a similar effect. Veterinary treatment usually necessitates drainage of the blood under general anaesthesia and also some method of stopping the dog shaking his head, to prevent further bleeding.

Arthritis is more likely to affect the older dog. *lynn@kipps.co.uk*

Do not feed your dog immediately after exercise, as this increases the risk of bloat.

David Tomlinson

BLOATED STOMACH

The rapid filling of the stomach with gas is a serious condition and can lead to death if urgent veterinary attention is not sought. It is seen in many deep-chested gundogs, often a few hours after feeding. A large meal fed when the dog is tired and hungry may lead to air being gulped down as the dog swallows food avidly. It is sensible not to feed the dog immediately after exercise, or to allow copious drinking of water at any one time. If in doubt, feed small pieces of food, dividing the ration through the day, while offering water in small amounts.

The signs of discomfort after a feed include: a gradual swelling of the abdomen, especially drum-like on the left side; pacing up and down; and trying to be sick, but only producing a little white froth. Contact the vet immediately; it may be that a stomach tube can relieve the bloat, but, in many cases, abdominal surgery is urgent, especially when the stomach has twisted in on itself.

BURNS AND SCALDS

First-aid measures require immediate cooling of the skin by pouring cold water over the burn repeatedly for at least 10 minutes. Some scalds, after hot water or oil have been spilt, penetrate the coat and may not be recognised until a large area of skin and hair peels away, since the heat has killed the surface skin cells. As these injuries are considered to be very painful, analgesics (pain relief) should be obtained, and, in anything but the smallest injured area, antibiotics would be advised, as secondary bacteria will multiply on exposed raw surfaces. Bandages and dressings are not a great help, but cling film has been used in some cases. Clipping the hair away from the area surrounding the burn and then flushing the injury with saline may be tolerated by the dog. An Elizabethan collar can be used to prevent the dog licking the area. In cases showing signs of serious shock, intravenous fluid therapy may be a necessity.

CALCULI (BLADDER STONES)

Bladder stones were often thought to be the cause of a dog seen straining to pass urine, but when these signs are seen, a veterinary examination for bladder inflammation (cystitis) or tumours is advised. Calculi are

All dog owners should acquire a basic knowledge of first-aid.

deposits of mineral salts from the urine, either in the neck of the bladder or nearer the base of the penis in the male. Stones can also form in the kidneys and these cause pain as they enter the ureters, but the bladder is not affected at first.

Calculi are recognisable on X-ray or with ultrasound examinations. The obstruction may be partial when the dog or bitch spends an unusually long time passing urine. Generally, in males they can become completely blocked and no urine can be voided; the dog strains, looking uncomfortable or in pain. An operation is usually necessary to remove calculi and diet advice will be given on how to avoid further attacks. Increasing the dog's water intake and providing opportunities for frequent

bladder emptying are important in prevention.

CANCER – CARCINOMA
The frequency of cancer in Weimaraners is no greater than any other breed, but, as dogs are now living longer, it may seem that more dogs are affected by tumours, especially in a dog's later years. One in every four dogs will be likely to have one of the many types of cancer during his lifetime. Skin lumps known as mast cell tumours should be watched for. These are seen as small nodules that may ulcerate and later spread to the lungs or other parts of the body unless diagnosed quickly.

CONSTIPATION
Unless the Weimaraner is known to have consumed large

quantities of bone or fibrous matter, straining may well be due to an enlarged prostate gland in the male or a foreign body in the rectum. Increasing the fluid intake and then medicating with liquid paraffin is advised, but if the problem persists, the vet should be visited.

CYSTITIS
Inflammation of the bladder is more common in the bitch and may first be noticed when the dog strains frequently with only small quantities of urine passed each time. Bladder calculi are fairly common in both sexes and will cause cystitis, but bacteria reaching the bladder from outside the body is the usual cause. In all cases the fluid intake should be reviewed, since a good 'wash through' of the bladder will

CATARACTS

Any opaqueness of the lens of the eye is termed a cataract. The dog may become blind and the eye takes on a pearl-like quality. Although cataracts are most commonly seen in old age or in dogs with diabetes, they can occur in young dogs following an injury (such as a thorn piercing the eye). Once the condition has been diagnosed, cataract surgery performed at specialised ophthalmic centres is very successful in suitably selected cases.

Conditions that affect the inside of the eye are more serious and can lead to blindness; the retina is the most important site of disease in the eye. Although not common, there is a group of inherited diseases, known as progressive retinal atrophy (PRA), which are known to occur in certain families. Blood tests are available for some breeds to identify the faulty genes.

reduce the risk of bacteria and mineral particles irritating the bladder lining. Medication with antispasmodics and an appropriate antibiotic will be required.

DIABETES

There are two sorts found in the dog, but 'sugar diabetes' (known as DM: diabetes mellitus) is seen most frequently in the older bitch. Caused by a lack of insulin to regulate the level of glucose in the blood, the signs include an increased thirst, passing large quantities of urine, eye cataracts and muscle weakness. It is associated with increased appetite and weight loss, as the dog attempts to satisfy the variations of his sugar levels. Diagnosis by urine and blood samples is followed by the injection of a suitable insulin

subcutaneously once or more daily.

Diabetes insipidus is uncommon in dogs and is related to the water control mechanism of the kidneys.

DISTEMPER

Fortunately now a rare virus infection, at one time distemper caused devastating illnesses. Routine vaccination has been very effective in preventing disease, but there is always the threat of a Weimaraner acquiring the infection if there has been a breakdown in the immune system. Affected dogs develop a high temperature, cough, diarrhoea and a purulent eye discharge. After several weeks, illness complications may still set in, with pneumonia or damage to the nervous system shown as nerve twitchings, paralysis or fits.

EPILEPSY AND FITS

Seizures occur relatively commonly in dogs and represent an acute and usually brief disturbance of normal electrical activity in the brain. They can be distressing for both the patient and the owner. Most fits last only a short time (less than two minutes) and owners will often telephone for veterinary advice once the seizure is over. Fits can sometimes occur close together and it is best to have the dog examined afterwards by a veterinary surgeon as soon as practical, even if the seizure has stopped. Some fits are prolonged or very frequent, and these may cause permanent brain damage. Once the fits have passed, the dog may seem dull or confused for several hours. Medication is used to control fits, but long-term treatment may be needed.

FRACTURES

Most broken bones are the result of some avoidable injury. An old dog with kidney disease may have brittle bones, but spontaneous fractures are quite rare even then. Treatment of fractures will require the attention of the vet, but there is little point in attempting first-aid as the dog will be in pain and will adopt the most comfortable position he can find. Natural painkillers known as endorphins come into action immediately following such an injury. If there is a skin wound associated with the fracture, this should be covered to reduce bacterial contamination, reducing the risk of osteomyelitis before the break in the bone can be satisfactorily repaired. X-rays will be necessary to confirm a crack or a major displacement of bones.

GASTRO-ENTERITIS

Vomiting is relatively common in dogs and can be a protective mechanism to try to prevent poisonous substances from entering the body. Gastro-enteritis includes attacks of diarrhoea, acting as a similar process to get rid of undesirable intestine contents by washing them out. The production of extra mucus and intestinal fluid is seen, with a rapid bowel evacuation movement. Both products of gastro-enteritis are objectionable; distressing to the dog and unpleasant for the owner who may have to clean up afterwards.

There are many causes, ranging from the simplest of the dog needing worming, to the complex interaction of viruses and bacteria that can cause an infection to spread through a kennel of dogs. A dietary diarrhoea may occur after any sudden change in food, scavenging, or an allergy to a particular food substance or additive. Where the signs of gastro-enteritis last more than 48 hours, a vet should be prepared to take samples and other tests to look for diseases such as pancreatitis, colitis or tumours (among many other possible causes), since some disorders may be life-threatening.

Treatment at home may be

If your dog is suffering from an upset stomach, withdraw food for a limited period but make sure that fresh water is freely available.

tried, using the principle of 'bowel rest': stopping feeding for 48 to 72 hours, fluids being allowed in repeated small quantities. Ice cubes in place of water may help to reduce vomiting. Electrolyte solutions, as are used in 'Traveller's Diarrhoea', will help with rehydration. Once the signs have alleviated, small feeds of smooth foods (such as steamed fish or chicken, with boiled rice) may be gradually introduced. Where there is continual diarrhoea for three to four weeks, the disease is unlikely to be resolved without a specific cause being identified and treated appropriately.

HEARTWORM DISEASE

Heartworms are still uncommon in the UK but are a major

problem in the USA where they are spread by mosquito bites. Dogs may be protected from six to eight weeks of age, with a monthly dose of the medication advised by the veterinarian. A blood test can be used to see if the heartworm antigen is present before commencing treatment, and this can be repeated annually. The filarial worms live in the heart and blood vessels of the lungs and cause signs such as tiring, intolerance of exercise and a soft, deep cough.

Heart failure leads to decline and an early death. There are many other disorders of heart valves and blood vessels, which cannot be described here, that cause a weakening of the heart muscle known as myocardial degeneration. A veterinary

Kennel cough spreads rapidly among dogs that live together.

cardiologist may be consulted for many heart disorders before a suitable treatment is found.

HEPATITIS

Inflammation of the liver may be due to a virus, but it is uncommon in dogs that have been protected with vaccines that also prevent the bacteria Leptospira from damaging the liver. Chronic liver disease may be due to heart failure, tumours or some type of toxicity. Dietary treatment may help if there are no specific medicines that can be used.

HIP DYSPLASIA

Hip dysplasia is an inherited disease of many working dogs. The breed mean score for Weimaraners is 13, lower than the score of many large dog breeds. It is possible to surgically treat a hip abnormality, but many cases can be controlled through regular exercise, muscle building, and the use of non-steroidal anti-inflammatory medication.

KENNEL COUGH

The signs of a goose-honking cough, hacking or retching that lasts for days to several weeks is due to damage at the base of the windpipe and bronchial tubes. The dry and unproductive cough is caused by a combination of viruses, bacteria and Mycoplasma. Vaccination is helpful in preventing the diseases, but may not give full protection, as strains of kennel cough seem to vary. The disease is highly contagious and spreads by droplets, so it may be acquired at dog shows or boarding kennels. An incubation period of five to seven days is usual. Veterinary treatments alleviate the cough and reduce the duration of the illness.

LEPTOSPIROSIS

Dogs that live in the country or swim in water may be more prone to this infection. Leptospira bacteria carried by rats can be found in pools and ditches where rodents have visited. Annual vaccination against the two types of Leptospira is advised. Treatment through antibiotics in the early stages is effective, but liver and kidney damage may permanently incapacitate the Weimaraner if the early signs with a fever are not recognised. Kidney and liver failure will lead to death. Antibiotic treatment for two to three weeks is needed to prevent the dog carrying Leptospira and infecting others.

LYME DISEASE BORRELIOSIS

This tick-borne disease affecting dogs, humans and, to a lesser extent, other domestic animals is common in the USA; it is also estimated that there may be a thousand cases a year in the UK. It is often seen as a sudden lameness with a fever, or, in the chronic form, one or two joints are affected with arthritis, often the carpus (wrist joint), which alerts the Weimaraner owner to this disease. Exposure to ticks (Ixodes ricinus in Britain) should raise suspicions if similar signs develop, especially if a rash appears around the bite and soon spreads. Treatment is effective and blood tests can be used to confirm Borrelia at the laboratory.

MANGE MITES

There are several mange types recognised to affect dogs, which may be the cause of scratching, hair loss and ear disease. Sarcoptic mange causes the most irritation and is diagnosed by skin scrapings or a blood test. Demodectic mange is a skin problem associated with close-coated breeds and is diagnosed by skin scrapes or from plucked hairs. It is probably transmitted from the bitch to the puppy when it first suckles, but may not show as skin disease for several months. Specific treatment is available from the vet, who should be consulted about any unusual skin rash or swellings. Otodectic mange occurs in the ears, and the mite can be found in the wax.

Cheyletiella is a surface mite of the coat; it causes white 'dandruff' signs and is diagnosed by coat brushing or sellotape impressions for microscope inspection. These mite infections first need identifying, but can then be treated with acaracide medication, such as amitraz, selamectin or imidacloprid and moxidectin provided by the vet. Traditional treatments required frequent bathing. It is essential to repeat the treatments after 10 to 14 days in order to prevent reinfestation.

NEPHRITIS

Dogs may suffer acute kidney failure after poisoning, obstructions to the bladder, or after shock with reduced blood supply. Chronic nephritis is more common in older dogs, where the blood accumulates waste products that the damaged kidneys cannot remove. The nephritic syndrome is caused by an immune-mediated damage within the kidney. The signs of increased thirst, loss of appetite and progressive weight loss are commonly seen with kidney

Dogs that live in rural areas are more likely to pick up ticks.

disease. Treatment of chronic renal failure is not reversible, but it aims to reduce the load on the remaining filter units (nephrons) and prevent further damage. Fluid intake should be encouraged, and if the dog is vomiting, intravenous drips will be needed to provide the liquid to help the kidneys work. Taking the dog outside frequently to encourage bladder emptying is helpful, too. Your vet can advise a special diet and will probably take repeated blood samples to monitor the kidneys' workload. If the ill Weimaraner does not eat, he will start drawing on his own body protein and the condition known as azotaemia will result with severe consequences. A diet of high biological value protein, low in phosphate but rich in vitamin B, should be given and diuretics to produce more urine

may be used in the nephritic syndrome cases.

OTITIS EXTERNA

Ear diseases are more common in dogs with earflaps that hang down. When a dog is suffering from otitis, strong-smelling discharge develops and the dog shakes his head or may show a head tilt. The repeated scratching and head shaking may cause a blood haematoma as a swelling underneath the skin of the ear flap. The presence of a grass seed in the ear canal should always be suspected in dogs that have been out in long grass during the summer; after becoming trapped, the seed can quickly work its way down the ear canal and can even penetrate the eardrum. The seed's spikes prevent it being shaken out of the ear and veterinary extraction of the seed is essential.

The Weimaraner, with its long earflaps, may be more prone to ear disease than dogs that have erect ear carriage.

PARVOVIRUS

This virus normally infects younger dogs and is most dangerous to the recently weaned puppy. Vaccination schedules are devised to protect susceptible dogs and the vet's advice should be taken as to when and how often a parvo vaccine should be used in your locality. The virus has an incubation of about three to five days and attacks the bowels with a sudden onset of vomiting and diarrhoea. Blood may be passed, dehydration sets in, and sudden death is possible.

Isolation from other puppies is essential, and the replacement of the fluids and electrolytes lost is urgent. Medication to stop the vomiting, antibiotics against secondary bacteria, and, later, a smooth, bland diet should be provided.

PYODERMA

This is a term used by some vets for a bacterial skin infection. It is a condition often seen in demodectic mange infections, but it is also associated with a wet, oozing skin condition known as 'wet eczema'. Juvenile pyoderma can occur in puppies between six and 16 weeks of age. The face swells and abscesses may form and burst, leaving scars unless given veterinary attention. Treatment for pyoderma should include: preventing licking and scratching, clipping away hair to encourage a dry surface where bacteria cannot multiply so readily, and giving an appropriate antibiotic. If the bacteria should tunnel inwards, the more difficult to treat furunculosis skin disorder will develop.

PYOMETRA

At one time pyometra was the commonest cause of illness in middle-aged to elderly bitches. This disease of the uterus would be seen in both bitches never bred from and those who had had litters born earlier in life. The cause is an imbalance of hormones that prepare the lining of the uterus for puppies, causing fluid and mucus to accumulate, leading to an acute illness if bacteria invade the organ. It is known as 'open pyometra' when a blood-stained mucoid discharge comes out, often sticking to the hairs around the vulva, and it has been confused with a bitch coming on heat unexpectedly. It can be more difficult to diagnose the cause of illness when there is no discharge present, and these cases are known as 'closed pyometra', where other ways of testing the patient for the uterus disorder may be employed by the vet. Although medical treatments are available, it is more usual to perform a hysterectomy, especially if the bitch has come to the end of her breeding career.

RINGWORM

Ringworm is a fungus disease of the skin that has nothing to do with worms, but it acquired the name from the circular red marks on the skin following infection. It may appear as bald, scaly patches and will spread to children or adults handling the dog unless precautions are taken. Treatments will vary depending on the extent of the problem.

VESTIBULAR DISEASE

Older Weimaraners may be vulnerable to a condition of a head tilt, often with the eye-flicking movements known as nystagmus. At one time it was commonly diagnosed as a 'stroke' because of its suddenness; the dog may circle or fall on one side, rolling, as he cannot balance. Vestibular disease develops suddenly, but, unlike the equivalent human stroke, there is no sign of bleeding nor of a vascular accident in the brain. Recovery may take place slowly, as the balance centre of the brain may regain its use after one to three weeks. Treatment by the vet will assist a return to normal, although some dogs always carry their head with a tilt.

INHERITED DISORDERS

Genetic defects and disorders have been a problem for a long time, but improved veterinary diagnostic methods and the fact that the longer dogs live, the

RABIES

This fatal virus infection is almost unknown in the UK but remains as a cause of death of animals and some humans in parts of the world where the preventive vaccine is not in regular use. Rabies attacks a dog's central nervous system and is spread by infective saliva. The disease usually follows a bite of an animal that is developing the virus. Annual rabies vaccination is an important way of controlling the disease.

more likely degenerative diseases are able to show themselves, means that perhaps undue emphasis has been placed on some inherited disorders. Healthy dogs should always be selected to breed from, and responsible Weimaraner breeders have done much to improve the breed and eliminate undesirable features.

EYE CONDITIONS

Cataracts are found in the breed and may be inherited. Entropion is an abnormality of the eyelids seen in younger dogs as an inward-turning of the lid, meaning that the lashes rub on the eyeball surface (the cornea), causing irritation and eye watering. Distichiasis and third eyelid eversion are examples of several eyelid problems of hereditary origin.

HIP DYSPLASIA

This is an inherited disease in many dogs, but the breed average score for the Weimaraner is at a

lower level than many other working breeds. Hip dysplasia disease is a malformation of both the femoral head and acetabulum 'cup' of the hip, which results in lameness, pain and eventual arthritic changes. X-rays can be taken to measure the joint structure and a score is awarded by a specialist after reading the photo plates. It is not a major problem in the breed, but anyone buying a puppy should enquire about the hip state of the parents before completing the purchase.

HYPOTHYROIDISM

A not uncommon condition in the breed, a low output of the thyroid hormone can lead to slowness in exercise, a dull, dry coat, and an unexplained increase of body weight. Hair loss, dark pigmentation and skin scales may also be found. Diagnosis will involve laboratory tests, and replacement therapy using thyroid tablets will restore the Weimaraner to his former

The Weimaraner is a breed without exaggeration and consequently suffers from relatively few inherited disorders.

energetic state. The disease may be present from birth or an immune-mediated inflammation of the thyroid gland in the neck.

PATELLAR LUXATION
The slipping out of place of the kneecap is often an inherited disease in active breeds, but it may also be the result of a torn ligament after jumping. Surgical operations are quite successful in curing the condition.

SYRINGOMYELIA
This uncommon disease is a malformation of the hindbrain fluids with fluid-filled cavities in the spinal cord of the upper neck. MRI screening tests are used from an early age to look for these defects. The disorder often shows up as a 'bunny hopping' gait, scratching of the shoulder region when the head position is altered, followed by pain. There is

no effective treatment and breeding should be avoided from suspect animals.

WOBBLER DISEASE
The syndrome results from an abnormality of the neck vertebrae, causing rear leg ataxia ('wobbling' walk) that may progress to paralysis of the hindquarters. Luxation of the atlanto axial joint of the spine at the top of the neck is another condition causing nerve pressure on the spinal column. Surgical treatment carried out by a veterinary specialist is available.

COMPLEMENTARY THERAPIES
There is a wide choice of treatments that can be given to dogs over and above the type of medical or surgical treatment that you might expect when

attending a veterinary surgery. Some of these alternative treatments have been proved to benefit dogs while others are better known for their effect on humans, where the placebo effect of an additional therapy has a strong influence on the benefit received.

PHYSIOTHERAPY
This is one of the longest-tested treatments used in injuries and after surgery on the limbs. Chartered physiotherapists and veterinary nurses who have studied the subject work under the direction of the vet, and are ready to advise or apply procedures that will help mobility and recovery. Massage, heat, exercise or electrical stimulation are used to relieve pain, regain movement and restore muscle strength.

HYDROTHERAPY

Hydrotherapy is very popular, as many dogs enjoy swimming. The use of water for the treatment of joint disease, injuries or for the maintenance of fitness and health is very effective.

ACUPUNCTURE

Acupuncture has a long history of healing. It is derived from Chinese medicine and involves the insertion of fine needles into specific locations in the body, known as 'acupuncture points'. The placing of the needles to stimulate nervous tissue is based on human charts and very good results have been reported when veterinary acupuncturists have selected suitable cases to treat.

REIKI

The laying on of a skilled operator's hands can have beneficial results. It is equally as convincing as acupuncture, and does not involve the dog tolerating needles in his body, but there are few qualified veterinary operators.

MAGNETIC THERAPY

Perhaps more questionable in observed results, magnetic therapy involves applying magnetic products to the dog, to relieve pain and increase mobility.

AROMATHERAPY

Aromatherapy also has a following. It involves the treatment of dogs with natural

An increasing number of dog owners are now turning to complementary therapies.

remedies, essential oils and plant extracts traditionally found in the wild.

PHYTOTHERAPY

Herbal medicine has proven benefits and there are an ever-increasing number of veterinary surgeons skilled in selecting appropriate plant products. Natural remedies are attractive to many users and provide a good alternative to a large number of conventional veterinary treatments. Herbal drugs have become increasingly popular and their use is widespread, but licensing regulations and studies on interactions between herbal products and other veterinary medicines are still incomplete. One treatment for kennel cough, with liquorice, thyme and echinacea, helped cure a dog in 24 hours without antibiotics.

As with all alternative therapies, it is necessary to consult a person who has the experience and specialised knowledge of applying the treatments. The Weimaraner's own vet should be informed, since there are contradictions between some veterinary medicines and other remedies. Acute and/or chronic liver damage has occurred after ingestion of some Chinese herbs and care in the application of 'natural products' is advised.

THE CONTRIBUTORS

THE EDITOR
PATSY HOLLINGS

Patsy Hollings came from a stock background, being a farmer's daughter and having horses all her life. She judged stock at young farmers club events nationally as did her husband, Stephen. In 1972, when Patsy and Stephen married and got their first dog, an English Setter, it was a natural progression to show her. In 1976, they bought their first Weimaraner, and soon after purchased a dog from the famous Hansom line of Dick Finch. With their knowledge of stock they have gone on to produce more than 60 UK champions. With advice, care and commitment they produced the record-holding brood bitch in the breed, Gunalt Joy. They owned/campaigned the breed's first Championship show Best in Show winner, Sh. Ch. Hansom Portman of Gunalt, bred the record Challenge Certificate holder, Sh. Ch.Gunalt Harris Tweed, and numerous group winners. Stephen and Patsy are the top Weimaraner breeders of all time in the UK and have also bred Champions in many countries throughout the world.

Patsy judges many breeds in the Gundog Group and all breeds Best in Show at Championship level. Patsy has judged in many counties around the world, including Australia, New Zealand, Barbados, South Africa, Scandinavia and Europe. These days Patsy leans more toward judging than exhibiting and among the highlights of her judging career are the Gundog Group at Crufts 2008 and Best in Show at South Wales, 2007. Patsy has written two books on Weimaraners and many articles on dogs, as well as appearing on television.

Stephen and Patsy attribute their great success to the fact that they are down to earth Yorkshire country folk, who know their strengths and therefore work together. This book and all the others could not have been without Stephens input, to which Patsy is grateful.
See Chapter Three: A Weimaraner for your Lifestyle, Chapter Four: The New Arrival, Chapter Five: The Best of Care and Chapter Seven: The Perfect Weimaraner.

KEVIN GREWCOCK
(RYANSTOCK)

Kevin Grewcock acquired his first Weimaraner, Ryan, in 1972, as a wedding present from his wife, Elaine. Since then Kevin and Elaine have established the successful Ryanstock affix. All of the Ryanstock dogs can be traced directly through a strong bitch line back to Kevin and Elaine's beloved Ryan. Ryanstock places great emphasis on breeding dogs that retain their working instincts.

Kevin and Elaine have also continued their love of showing, with some considerable successes. Almost one quarter of the dogs they have bred have qualified for entry in the Kennel Club stud book. They have also produced 11 Junior Warrant winners, a new Show certificate of merit winner and have made up many Show Champions, with titles gained in each of the last three decades.

Kevin began judging Weimaraners in 1977 and now judges all Gundog breeds at Open Shows. At Championship level Kevin awarded Challenge Certificates in Weimaraners for the first time in 1986. The highlight of his judging career so far was being asked by the Kennel Club to judge the breed at Crufts in 2000.

Kevin and Elaine continue to enthusiastically work their dogs throughout the shooting season, and currently share their home with seven Weimaraners.
See Chapter One: Getting to Know Weimaraners.

JEAN FAIRLIE (TASAIRGID)

With a background in Bloodhounds, Jean and Allan bought their first Weimaraner from Patsy and Stephen Hollings in 1978. Gunalt Winter Will o' the Wisp was the first Gunalt Weimaraner ever to be shown and so they were hooked on this special breed. Thus was born the Tasairgid affix. Pronounced 'Tasherikit', it is a corruption of the Gaelic for Grey Ghost, the Weimaraner's nickname.

Next came Ch. Bredebeck Ilka (Emma) the first Show Champion bitch in Scotland. She won a triple Junior Warrant, 9 CCs, 13 Res. CCs, Best of Breed Crufts 1984 and WCGB Brood Bitch 1986. Jean and Emma

tramped the moors with a local shooting sybdicate. Her instinct was natural. It had to be – Jean knew virtually nothing. There is such a rush of pride in watching this beautiful dog performing the work she was bred for – a true Hunt Point Retriever Weimaraner with the beauty for the show ring.

Next came the babies. Emma's first litter, by Aylmarch Aldous of Tasairgid, produced Sh. Ch. Tasairgid Deep Secret JW. Her second, by Ch. Ragstone Ryuhlan, produced Ch. Tasairgid Talked About. Her third, and last, by Colsidex Yankee at Gamepoint, produced Tasairgid Prime Candidate, 1CC, 2 Res. CCs and BIS WCGB Champ Show and Tasairgid Grade A-Plus, who in turn produced Sh. Ch. Tasairgid Ultra Easy.

Jean was the first person in Scotland approved to award Challenge Certificates in Weimaraners and Hungarian Vizslas and she judged Weimaraners at Crufts 2008.
See Chapter Two: The First Weimaraners.

JULIA BARNES

Julia has owned and trained a number of different dog breeds, and is a puppy socialiser for Dogs for the Disabled. A former journalist, she has written many books, including several on dog training and behaviour. Julia is indebted to Patsy Hollings for her specialist knowledge of Weimaraners.
See Chapter Six: Training and Socialisation.

DICK LANE BScFRAgSFRCVS

Dick qualified from the Royal Veterinary College and spent most of his time in veterinary practice in Warwickshire. He had a particular interest in assistance dogs: working for the Guide Dogs for the Blind Association and more recently for Dogs for the Disabled as a founder Trustee. Dick has been awarded a Fellowship of the Royal College of Veterinary Surgeons and a Fellowship of the Royal Agricultural Societies. He has recently completed an Honours BSc in Applied Animal Behaviour and Training, awarded by the University of Hull.
See Chapter Eight: Happy and Healthy.

USEFUL ADDRESSES

BREED CLUBS

To obtain up-to-date contact information for the following breed clubs, please contact the Kennel Club:

- Weimaraner Association
- North of England Weimaraner Society
- Weimaraner Club of Great Britain
- Weimaraner Club of Scotland.

KENNEL CLUBS

American Kennel Club (AKC)
5580 Centerview Drive
Raleigh, NC 27606
Telephone: 919 233 9767
Fax: 919 233 3627
Email: info@akc.org
Web: www.akc.org

The Kennel Club (UK)
1 Clarges Street
London, W1J 8AB
Telephone: 0870 606 6750
Fax: 0207 518 1058
Web: www.the-kennel-club.org.uk

TRAINING AND BEHAVIOUR

Association of Pet Dog Trainers
PO Box 17
Kempsford, GL7 4W7
Telephone: 01285 810811
Email: APDToffice@aol.com
Web: http://www.apdt.co.uk

Association of Pet Behaviour Counsellors
PO BOX 46
Worcester, WR8 9YS
Telephone: 01386 751151
Fax: 01386 750743
Email: info@apbc.org.uk
Web: http://www.apbc.org.uk/

ACTIVITIES

Agility Club
http://www.agilityclub.co.uk/

British Flyball Association
PO Box 109, Petersfield, GU32 1XZ
Telephone: 01753 620110
Fax: 01726 861079
Email: bfa@flyball.org.uk
Web: http://www.flyball.org.uk/

Working Trials
36 Elwyndene Road, March, Cambridgeshire, PE15 9RL
Web: www.workingtrials.co.uk

World Canine Freestyle Organisation
P.O. Box 350122, Brooklyn, NY 11235-2525, USA
Telephone: (718) 332-8336
Fax: (718) 646-2686
Email: wcfodogs@aol.com
Web: www.worldcaninefreestyle.org

HEALTH

Alternative Veterinary Medicine Centre, Chinham House, Stanford in the Vale, Oxfordshire, SN7 8NQ
Email: enquiries@bahvs.com
Web: www.bahvs.com

British Association of Veterinary Ophthalmologists (BAVO)
Email: hjf@vetspecialists.co.uk or secretary@bravo.org.uk
Web: http://www.bravo.org.uk/

British Small Animal Veterinary Association
Woodrow House, 1 Telford Way, Waterwells Business Park, Quedgeley, Gloucestershire, GL2 2AB
Telephone: 01452 726700
Fax: 01452 726701
Email: customerservices@bsava.com
Web: http://www.bsava.com/

British Veterinary Hospitals Association
Station Bungalow, Main Rd, Stocksfield, Northumberland, NE43 7HJ
Telephone: 07966 901619
Fax: 07813 915954
Email: office@bvha.org.uk
Web: http://www.bvha.org.uk/

Royal College of Veterinary Surgeons (RCVS)
Belgravia House, 62-64 Horseferry Road, London, SW1P 2AF
Telephone: 0207 222 2001
Fax: 0207 222 2004
Email: admin@rcvs.org.uk
Web: www.rcvs.org.uk

ASSISTANCE DOGS

Canine Partners
Mill Lane, Heyshott, Midhurst, West Sussex, GU29 0ED
Telephone: 08456 580480
Web: www.caninepartners.co.uk

Dogs for the Disabled
The Frances Hay Centre, Blacklocks Hill, Banbury, Oxon, OX17 2BS
Telephone: 01295 252600
Web: www.dogsforthedisabled.org

Guide Dogs for the Blind Association
Burghfield Common, Reading, RG7 3YG
Telephone: 01189 835555
Web: www.guidedogs.org.uk/

Hearing Dogs for Deaf People
The Grange, Wycombe Road, Saunderton, Princes Risborough, Bucks, HP27 9NS
Telephone: 01844 348100
Web: www.hearingdogs.org.uk

Pets as Therapy
3 Grange Farm Cottages, Wycombe Road, Saunderton, Princes Risborough, Bucks, HP27 9NS
Telephone: 01844 345445
Web: http://www.petsastherapy.org/

Support Dogs
21 Jessops Riverside, Brightside Lane, Sheffield, S9 2RX
Tel: 0870 609 3476
Web: www.support-dogs.org.uk

Sponsor a guide dog puppy for just £1 a week

SPONSOR
A PUPPY APPEAL

To find out more, please call
0870 240 6993*
please quote reference PBAC
or go to
www.sponsorapuppy.org.uk

Guide Dogs